The Magic of Music

Richard Baker

The Magic of Music

HAMISH HAMILTON
LONDON

This book was designed and produced by
George Rainbird Ltd
Marble Arch House
44 Edgware Road
London w 2

Published in Great Britain in 1975 by
Hamish Hamilton Ltd
90 Great Russell Street
London WC1B 3PT

House editor: Yorke Crompton
Picture research: Victoria Nicolson and
    John Henderson
Indexing: Ellen Crampton
Design: Jonathan Gill-Skelton

Filmset, printed, and bound in Great Britain
by Cox & Wyman Ltd, Fakenham, Norfolk

ISBN 0 241 89194 9

Contents

Colour Plates

For Andrew and James,
David, Janie and Michael

Sixteenth-century performers practising the magic of music

I
Theme

'Music produces a kind of pleasure which human nature cannot do without.' That statement was made by the Chinese philosopher Confucius some five hundred years before the birth of Christ, and it is some indication of how universal, and how ancient, is the art of music. The aim of this book is to provide an all-round introduction to the subject for those who are just beginning to experience its unique pleasures.

Nowadays people have the opportunity to make music very early in life, and can sometimes produce quite astonishing results with the right kind of teaching; but, generally speaking, we do not arrive at any conscious awareness of what music means to us until the early teens, when we are beginning to enter the world of adult feeling in every way. Then, if we are sensitive to music at all, it may overwhelm us like a great wave, and we begin to wonder what this wonderful thing is all about. Older listeners may come to enjoy classical music through having first been moved by drama, 'pop' or jazz.

Mind you, for the young, there is sometimes a conflict between this growing sense of joy in music and the hard slog of learning to sing, or to play a musical instrument – and there must be many, fettered to a piano stool when others are out playing football, who (like myself in those conditions) have felt strongly that music is a pleasure human nature can well do without. But these are incidental troubles: nothing worth while was ever achieved without effort, and the reward of being able to make music, particularly in company with others, is beyond price.

Making music, in fact, is the very best way of learning about music. The next best way is listening to it. In my view, there's nothing quite like going to a concert and sharing in the unique and unrepeatable experience of a live performance. But nowadays the record player has reached such a degree of perfection that it provides the main road to music for vast numbers of people; indeed, with good reproduction, the details of a score are often heard with greater clarity on a gramophone record than they are in the opera house or concert hall. Radio too, of course, is a most important medium for music, provided it can be heard without too much interference. And television, already used with great resource and imagination in the field of musical appreciation, is likely to become even more significant as a means of transmitting music itself when ways are found of improving the sound-quality of the television receiver, or of linking it to stereo equipment in the home: methods of doing this are already being developed.

Access to music, whether for the listener or the participant, is much easier now than it was a generation ago. Radio, television, and the gramophone are readily available for most people. And the spread of active musical groups has been sensational, with an astonishing improvement in musical standards. To take one instance, the growth of the youth orchestra movement around the world in the years since the Second World War has proved that youthful enthusiasm, well guided, can sometimes almost prove a match for the great professional orchestras, certainly in terms of musical excitement – and that, to my mind, is one of the things music is really about.

Nowadays, fortunately, the academic aspect of music has been put in its place in teaching the young: the first priority is to generate enthusiasm and enjoyment. And how right this is! Technical proficiency must be acquired, particularly in our complex 'Western' music, but we must never lose sight of the fact that music is essentially a spontaneous thing, perhaps the most potent means of expression available to the human spirit, going beyond words to give voice to an inner need for sound and rhythm.

Many exciting things have happened in our own times in the world of music, reminding us of its essential nature. Though some of the newest developments are hard to follow, and some probably lead up blind alleys, composers in many countries are experimenting with completely fresh techniques – making use of the electronic equipment now available, for instance – and they have broken away from the conventional symphony orchestra as the accepted medium for their most significant works. In our century, composers have also drawn increasingly for inspiration on sources of music beyond the European tradition; they have made use, for example, of African and South American rhythms, Indian instruments, and the traditional music of Indonesia or Japan, and have gone back to the inexhaustible freshness of folk music in its multitudinous variety around the world.

In other words, in the 1970s, we are in a position to see that the music of the 'great composers' of the West is only one way of making music. The snobbery that once divided 'popular' from 'classical' music is happily dying, and we acknowledge that the playing of a shepherd on his reed-pipe, the strident song of the Spanish gypsy, the improvised blues of the jazz musician can have just as valid a musical message as the great symphony.

This book is an attempt to convey with relatively few words and many pictures what music means around the world and, against this background, how it grew and developed in the West. Naturally I have devoted a good deal of space to those European creators of music who have given us our noblest experience of the art; but it's my belief that music, in one form or another, is for every man. And my hope for this book is that it may help in some small way to sharpen the 'pleasure which human nature cannot do without'.

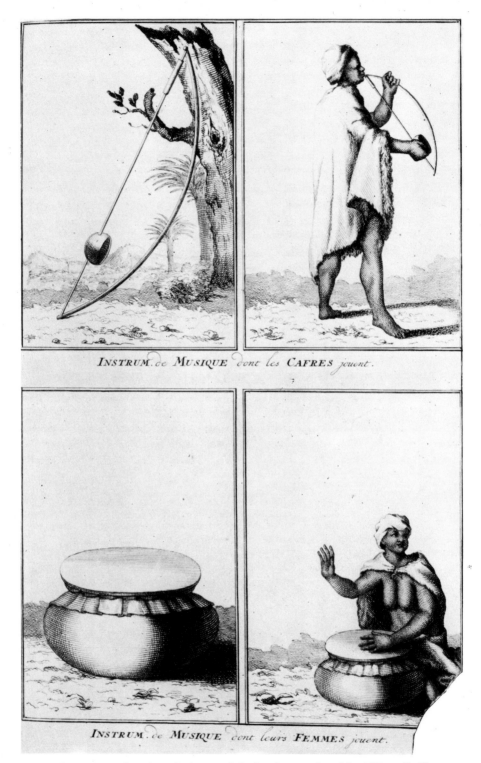

INSTRUM. de MUSIQUE dont les CAFRES jouent.

INSTRUM. de MUSIQUE dont leurs FEMMES jouent.

Instruments, based on the bow and the bowl, once played by African Kaffirs

2

Variations

How and where did music begin?

The fact is that no one knows, any more than anyone really knows how and where life began. In spite of everything the scientists have told us, the origin of life remains a mystery. And from its very beginnings music has been closely identified with the meaning, and the mystery, of life.

Imagine yourself living, not in a comfortable house with shops and supermarkets not too far away where you can buy food and clothing, but in some roughly constructed shelter or, if you're lucky, a dry cave. Every bit of food you require you must grow or hunt for yourself, in a more or less hostile environment without artificial light or heat, without any of the thousand and one tools we have devised, over the centuries, to make life more bearable.

In this vulnerable situation, men have few means of defending themselves against the elements. When the thunder crashes out and the lightning strikes, when the volcano explodes and earthquakes heave, when flood and drought alternately ruin crops, primitive human beings are apt to feel that nature is full of mighty and mysterious powers they do not understand, and which somehow must be appeased if life is to be tolerable at all. The human voice was probably already able to produce shrill hunting cries, often in imitation of the calls of animals, and it is easy to imagine such cries being developed into some kind of invocation to the capricious god of the chase, into what may have been chanted prayer. And here, perhaps, lie the early beginnings of what we now know as song.

And then someone, perhaps, accidentally struck a certain stone in a certain way, and found that it made a pleasant sound; someone else twanged the string of his hunting bow and liked the noise it made; and someone discovered that if he blew down a piece of hollow bamboo it developed a voice of its own. By such means, instrumental music may have begun to come to life.

But the discovery of song and the creation of musical instruments both owed their origin to a human impulse which lies much deeper than conscious intention: the need for rhythm in life. Just as day follows night, the tides advance and recede, the moon waxes and wanes and the seasons succeed one another, so the human organism responds to rhythm. The need is a deep one, transcending thought, and disregarded at our peril. Our earliest ancestors were instinctively aware of the need; and so, at a very early date, rhythmic actions and rhythmic songs, together with a

growing number of instruments whose voices must themselves have
seemed at first mysterious, were used to bring man into contact with the
mysteries of life. Music, in fact, was the magic by which the human hoped
to attune himself to the superhuman.

But of course this is not the only sort of music, though there is less
evidence of other kinds to be found in history; for, while history often
records details of musical ceremonies, the more spontaneous activities of
the human race are frequently forgotten, and from the beginnings of time
people no doubt made music spontaneously, because they were happy or
sad, just as we do today.

The first strong evidence of civilization emerges from the Middle East,
from the lands between the rivers Tigris and Euphrates, in what is now
Iraq and was once called Mesopotamia; and that evidence tells us there
was music in Mesopotamia six thousand years ago. There was probably
music for enjoyment; without doubt there was music in religious ceremonies, for we know of a reed-pipe whose sound was related (in flattery
perhaps) to the breath of the thunder-god, and of a drum identified with
Ea, ruler of the deep, whose tendency to produce disastrous floods had to
be discouraged somehow. Excavation has revealed evidence of quite
elaborate rituals in the temples of Sumeria (*c.* 4000–3000 B.C.) which made
use of specially trained singers and a considerable variety of instruments,
including a vertical flute, tambourine, lyre and two kinds of harp, one of
which was probably the result of adding extra strings to a hunter's bow.
During the five hundred years of Babylonian rule (*c.*1830–1270 B.C.) the
use of music in temple services was much extended, and certain Babylonian psalm-tunes found their way into the Jewish tradition and so into
the music of the early Christian Church. It is not until Assyrian times
(*c.*1270–606 B.C.) that we begin to hear much of music-making outside
the temples; but we know that the Assyrian rulers engaged musicians as
part of the royal household, and that the court minstrel now became a
figure of some importance.

Echoes of music are often to be heard in the resounding words of the
Old Testament, and a memorable passage in the Book of Daniel describes
the large band employed in the image-worship of King Nebuchadnezzar
II (604–562 B.C.). This included the horn, pipes, the lyre, and harps,
together forming a *sumfonyah* (which sounds remarkably like our modern
symphony). It was during this Chaldean period that a theory of music
emerged which was closely connected with astrology and mathematics,
and which was to have a profound influence on the development of music
in Europe. Chaldean philosophers expressed the ancient belief, widely
shared around the world, that a perfect harmony exists throughout the
universe, and that man in his music-making should attempt to come as
close to it as possible. These ideas passed into the musical theory of Egypt
and, through the Greek philosopher Pythagoras (sixth century B.C.),
into the ideas of classical Greece and ultimately of Europe in general –

ABOVE Yehudi Menuhin,
violin, and Ravi Shankar, *sitar*,
with players of the *tabla* and
baya (drums) and *tamboura*.
LEFT In China: a herdsman
playing a Tibetan lute

a story we shall take up again a little later. At this point, we follow the
early traces of music further East.

The subcontinent of INDIA is so vast, and so varied in tradition, that
it is dangerous to generalize about any aspect of Indian culture. The
origins of Indian music undoubtedly go far back into antiquity, particularly in south-eastern India, where the Tamil people believed that the
world issued from the tambourine of God, and where the cult of nature
worship may have given rise to the belief that the notes of the Indian scale
are based on the cries of animals. To the north-west, India was open to a
succession of invasions. We know that a people of Mesopotamian origin
flourished in the Indus valley as early as 2500 B.C. and enjoyed music and
dancing. They were succeeded by Aryan-speaking peoples whose elaborate religious rituals were laid down in the four books called Vedas, and
the first of them, the Rig Veda, produced about 1500 B.C., established rules
for temple chanting which are still observed in many parts of India; the
third book, the Sama Veda, dealt with a less austere form of chanting and
established a musical scale which can still be heard in some northern
areas of the country.

In ancient Indian music, the voice was considered supremely important, for it was thought to represent the 'union of audible sound and
intellect' (though instruments, too, were mentioned in the Vedas) and
the ancient Sanskrit word for music, *samgita*, stood for the 'art and science
of singing with music and dancing'. The Vedic traditions were embodied
in Hindu religious ceremonies, in which dancing according to intricate
rules continued to be of great significance, and Nataraja, Lord of the
Dance, became an important Hindu deity. But a distinction was drawn
between the two kinds of music: *marga* was sacred music, which, if correctly performed, could lead to the liberation of the human spirit; *desi*
was music designed to entertain.

Between about 250 B.C. and A.D. 600, Greek ideas (through the invasion
of Alexander the Great) and the spread of Buddhism both influenced
Indian music, and it was not until the early Middle Ages, when Hinduism
again established its ascendancy, that the theory of Indian music was
expressed in words. Indian classical theory, like our own, recognizes a
scale of eight notes (the octave) and seven intervals; but these intervals
are subdivided not like ours into semitones, but into twenty-two *srutis*, of
more or less equal size, which can be grouped together in various ways
to produce quite different effects.

The basic form of melody in Indian classical music is the *raga*, a word
which literally means 'colour' or 'feeling'. There must have been a great
variety of moods and feelings in ancient India, for the Tamils are said to
have known some twelve thousand ragas. Nowadays a hundred and thirty-
two are generally recognized and about half are generally used. They are
connected with certain hours of the day, seasons of the year, and other
landmarks in life, and express the appropriate mood through using

The harp in ancient Egypt

different groups of notes in special ways that are felt to correspond.

The raga is performed in association with a prescribed *tala* or time-measure. These talas again vary considerably in character, and are often very complex. And there is a third element, rather like the sustained note, or 'drone', of the bagpipe; it consists of four notes which are sounded right through the piece, regardless of what else is happening. This is called *kharaja* and is supposed to contribute a timeless, eternal element to the piece.

There is certainly a timeless atmosphere at a performance of Indian music. Trained Indian musicians share a common knowledge of a great range of ragas and talas. Their improvised performances, not unlike those of good jazz musicians, though within more tightly prescribed rules, may well last an hour and a half and, to the trained ear, bring a long succession of subtle delights. Even to one who knows little of Indian music, the sound of the *sitar* or the *vina*, together with the *tambura* (which provides the 'drone') and Indian drums, can be very seductive; in more recent times the violin, too, has often been used in Indian music-making, and Yehudi Menuhin (b. 1916) is only one of a number of distinguished Western musicians who have felt the great attraction of Indian music either through sharing in performances or as a source of inspiration in composition.

The legendary emperors of ancient CHINA are each said to have had a musical system, but it is not until the Shang or Yin Dynasty (*c.* 1766–1122 B.C.) that any real evidence of musical activity emerges: we know they used a *ch'ing* (a kind of stone) and a *hsuan* (a globe-shaped flute) among other instruments, and from a book of songs of a slightly later date we learn of choirs of boys and girls singing alternate sections of a song, and by so doing representing the two opposed principles of the universe: Yang, which can be roughly equated with maleness, and Yin, which incorporates the female qualities. It was thought that harmony in life could only result from a reunion of these two principles, and that music could help to achieve this.

From the earliest known period, musical sounds were associated in Chinese tradition with the essence of life, and when musical theory came to be defined, at much the same time as the Chaldean philosophers were defining it in Mesopotamia, there once again emerged the concept of a natural harmony in the universe, to which man must try to attune himself. Confucius (551–479 B.C.) edited a number of ancient Chinese books which contain many references to music.

At the core of Chinese musical theory is a single foundation-note known as *huang chung* ('yellow bell'), which legend says was first established by cutting a piece of bamboo so as to produce the 'pitch of a man's voice when he spoke without passion'. But in fact the yellow bell had to be re-established for each dynasty, and such importance was attached to doing this correctly that an Imperial Office of music was set up; one of its

A mounted drummer in Nigeria

ABOVE A Yugoslav peasant with his gusle,
a traditional instrument.
LEFT Flute-playing by a Komu-So priest
in Japan

principal jobs was to standardize musical pitch. If the correct pitch was not established, it was believed that political chaos would ensue.

From the yellow bell were generated *lü*, a series of twelve notes, which were more or less linked with the twelve hours of the clock and the twelve months of the year, and each of these notes became the basis for a five-note ('pentatonic') scale, which incidentally also exists in the folk music of the American continent, reinforcing the notion of an Asiatic invasion of America in remote times.

Chinese instruments were mainly of the percussion type (drums, bells, gongs, cymbals and the rest) until Buddhist monks, who reached China from India in the early centuries of the Christian era, introduced the *ch'in*, a kind of zither; it was at this period, too, that dancing became important in religious ceremonies. By the time of the Sung Dynasty (A.D. 960–1279) such ceremonies had become extremely elaborate, employing as many as two hundred and forty zithers, two hundred mouth-organs and twenty oboes as well as various gongs and drums, not to mention a large choir. These musicians produced no harmony or melody in our sense of the words, but a luminous glow of sound, continuous yet ever changing, with a constant succession of subtle iridescent effects, a kind of music which, in the words of Confucius, is 'mild and delicate, and keeps a uniform mood', thus helping to induce a calm nobility in the mind of man.

Beyond the temple walls, music was of great importance in the Chinese court over many centuries, and during the Sung Dynasty the first hints of Chinese opera begin to appear. This form of art was to become enormously elaborate under the Ming emperors (A.D. 1368–1644). Men played the female parts as well as the male; there would be as many as a hundred acts, with song and spoken dialogue alternating. Among orchestral instruments the *p'i p'a*, or short lute, was used, together with flutes, guitars, organs and oboes, and there were important interludes for percussion. The mouth-organ, by the way, was brought into Europe from China in the eighteenth century and inspired a whole family of Western instruments, including the accordion and harmonium, which work on the same vibrating-reed principle.

Opera is still a highly popular form of entertainment in Communist China today, but musically it now owes a great deal to Western influence, both in form and instrumentation, and the stories are generally full of propaganda, though the unique quality of Chinese traditional music is still recognized and preserved by scholars and musicians.

In the last hundred years, JAPAN has rapidly assimilated Western ways in music as in so many other spheres of life, and Japanese performers practise the art as efficiently as Japanese engineers make cars or transistor radios. And contemporary composers manage to give their work a distinctive quality by introducing some of the feeling of traditional Japanese music, though in fact this tradition has always been subject to strong outside influence, notably from China and India in earlier years.

However, at least two Japanese instruments, the *yamato-bue*, or national flute, and the *yamato-goto*, the national zither, are thought to date back to the Stone Age, before metal, together with foreign ways, was brought to Japan from China in the first century A.D. These instruments are associated with the legend of the goddess Amaterasu, who was summoned by a godlike zither from her cave to bring light, dance and music to the world, a story which inspired the musical ceremony of the Shinto religion known as *kagura*.

To a great extent through the activities of Buddhist priests, both Indian and Chinese musical forms had become well established in Japan by the eighth century, at which time the ruling emperor followed another Chinese example by establishing an imperial office of music. In the early Middle Ages, the nobility developed an aristocratic form of musical art known as *gagaku*, which included both orchestral music and highly formal court dancing; but it was not until the so-called Age of the Warriors, or Samurai, which lasted from the thirteenth to the seventeenth century, that Japanese traditional music began to assume its most characteristic forms.

Early in this period there emerged the so-called No plays (*no* means 'talent'), of which some three hundred are still acted. They portray a mixture of religious and everyday stories, intoned by actor-singers together with a chorus accompanied by a flute and three kinds of drum. To these instruments a type of guitar called *samisen* is now added, thanks to the influence of a more popular form of No drama called Kabuki. Such entertainments are performed according to the most rigid conventions and sound very shrill and strange to foreign ears, though moments of high drama come across with shattering power.

With the decline of martial influence, the seventeenth and eighteenth centuries brought a gentler kind of music, and the *samisen* was joined by an instrument now thought of as the national instrument of Japan. This is the *koto*, a large zither some six and a half feet long with thirteen strings which is laid on the floor and played by a performer who squats before it. It is used either as a solo instrument or to accompany the voice. Koto music is based on a series of five-note scales, rather similar to the Chinese system, but producing a sound uniquely characteristic of Japan.

Many Far Eastern countries have musical styles which are to some extent individual, but none is more striking than that of INDONESIA, where the sound of the *gamelan* orchestra is deeply rooted in the way of life of South-East Asia. This depends largely on the cultivation of rice, and from very early times the sound made by wood striking on wood was familiar to village women as they pounded the rice after harvesting. It was this sound, perhaps, which led, over the years, to the development of that typically Indonesian instrument, the xylophone. And in parts of Java a natural instrument lay to hand in the piece of tilting bamboo used to irrigate the terraced paddy fields, which made a pleasing 'clunk' on a

An Indonesian percussion orchestra

stone as it resumed its normal position. People in those parts must have appreciated the sound, for they made bamboos of different sizes to produce notes of different pitch; and when they sounded together a very attractive effect was produced.

It was from such beginnings that the gamelan orchestra began to develop in the early Middle Ages: an orchestra which consists largely of percussion instruments including drums, celestas, xylophones and various chiming devices, with the addition, in some cases, of the *suling* (a kind of flute) and the *rebab* (the spike-fiddle). Such orchestras were, and are, used on all kinds of occasions. Among the most interesting are performances of the ancient shadow-plays of Java, and the superb ritual dance-dramas of Bali.

Gamelan music is based on two different scales, *pelog* and *slendro*. As each requires a different tuning, there are two kinds of gamelan orchestra, together with a third, the 'royal' gamelan, which can play compositions written alternately in the two styles. The effect of gamelan music is very strange to Western ears, for both scales are very different from ours, the pelog scale having five notes irregularly spaced over the range of our octave, while each tone in the slendro scale has a value equal to about one and one-fifth of the tones in our system. The shimmering texture of the music is, however, very attractive, and it has fascinated a number of composers. Among them was Debussy, who heard gamelan music at the Paris Exhibition of 1889. Benjamin Britten has made use of many 'chime' instruments in his ballet *The Prince of the Pagodas*.

The influence of Indonesian music must have travelled in ancient days across the Indian Ocean to AFRICA, for there we find a number of instruments of the xylophone type, particularly in the coastal regions which would have been most likely to be exposed to Indonesian visitors. Naturally, in so vast a continent, a great number of different musical influences can be traced (the Arab tradition is of great importance in many areas) and, as in the case of India, it is hardly possible to generalize with any accuracy.

However, it does seem broadly true that African music is of the traditional type, handed down from generation to generation, and has not been subject, like the music of India and China, to the codes of musical theorists, at least until the relatively modern passion for folk-music collecting began. In Africa, as elsewhere, from the very earliest time, musical sounds were thought to have supernatural powers, and funerals in West Africa are still accompanied by the tinkling of bells to indicate the passage of the soul to the kingdom of death. In some parts of Africa, the royal drums are treated with superstitious reverence and accorded ritual worship: not even the ruler himself is allowed to silence them, so it is clear they are regarded as embodying an eternal principle beyond human control. Such royal drums are sometimes played in batteries of a dozen or so, and the performance calls for great skill.

The rhythm of the drum

There is of course a great variety of African musical instruments, among them harps derived originally, perhaps, from hunting bows; flutes of various types, some thought to possess special magical qualities; and ceremonial trumpets and horns fashioned from ivory. There is also magnificent choral singing and chanting of great variety in many African communities; but the drum remains the supreme African instrument. It is played not only in many shapes and sizes, ranging from the royal drums themselves down to small drums held in the crook of an arm, but also in a great variety of situations, not least important as an instrument of communication. 'Talking' drums are still used for communication over long distances and are capable of great subtlety, for they use wide variations of pitch and rhythm and can be so eloquent that even those not familiar with spoken language in those parts of the world feel they can understand the message of the drums.

That message of vibrant, vital rhythm crossed the Atlantic with the slaves to the American continent, where it bore fruit ultimately in jazz, in the calypsos and steel bands of the Caribbean and the frenetic abandon of the Rio Carnival; while the African choral tradition gave rise to one of the most expressive of all kinds of music, the Negro spiritual, reflecting as it does the anguish of the exiled human soul.

Now let us return to the part of the world where we began to trace the story of music: the Middle East. There, a people whose songs have often been songs of exile – the JEWS – lived a nomadic life in the desert while the

A Riff sounding a Moroccan horn

empires of Mesopotamia and Egypt were at their height. About 2000 B.C., Abraham led them from the Mesopotamian city of Ur into Palestine; however, his grandson Jacob took them into Egypt in search of pasture, and there they became slaves. It was only after some four hundred years that Moses brought them back into Palestine and a more settled life could begin.

Until that time, the principal Jewish instruments were the timbrel or tabret (a small drum), the lyre and the flute, while a *hazozra* (a trumpet) and *shofar* (a ram's horn) were used as signals at significant moments. The ram's horn is the only instrument found in Jewish synagogues to this day, and is said to have acquired its special religious importance from the story of the ram which Abraham sacrificed instead of his son Isaac.

Music played a great part in the early story of Israel. We have all read how the young David soothed Israel's first king, Saul (1050–1013 B.C.), with his playing of the lyre, and when he in turn became King, it was David himself, poet, composer and performer, who danced before the Ark, organized the music in the Temple and appointed the Levites as a caste of sacred musicians. Two hundred and forty-eight Levites, we are told, sang and played their instruments at the dedication of King Solomon's Temple, and for some four centuries this splendour continued. In the sixth century B.C., King Nebuchadnezzar conquered Jerusalem, and many Jews spent forty years in exile in Babylon; but after this, in the period of the second Temple, music again played a dominant role. At this time began the practice of alternate chanting of the scriptures by priest and people, and later it was adopted by the Christian Church. In fact, the rituals of the Hebrew Temple greatly influenced the Christian liturgy in its early days, while at much the same period Roman persecution in Palestine drove many Jews to seek refuge in other lands, taking with them, to some degree, their musical traditions.

In succeeding centuries, the Jews established themselves throughout most of Europe, though it was in Eastern Europe, where they developed a whole range of impassioned popular songs, that their musical influence was perhaps most strongly felt, with its powerful undercurrent of nostalgia. The synagogues carried on the ancient Temple practice of chanting passages from the Bible, and the chanting of prayers became a highly developed art, with the *hazan* (precentor) embellishing the standard melodies in elaborate fashion. But the more influential the Jewish communities of Europe became, the more they adopted the style, musical and otherwise, of their adopted lands, and famous Jewish composers such as Mendelssohn and Meyerbeer, Offenbach and Mahler, produced music which is in no special way Jewish in character. Nowadays, in Israel itself, musicians and scholars are engaged in retracing the true traditions of Jewish music-making, before they became totally blurred with other influences. But perhaps the most distinctive Jewish contribution to the art has been in the performance of music: many of the most outstanding conductors and virtuosi have been Jews.

In most of the musical traditions we have so far discussed, we come across more evidence of sacred music in early times than of music for personal enjoyment. An exception is the ARAB WORLD, whose earliest recorded history contains references to the singing girls who provided court entertainment. Sensuous dancing was part of the entertainment too, with the accompaniment of such instruments as drums, tambourines, harps and lutes, so it is perhaps no surprise that the great religious leader Mohammed (A.D. 571–632) numbered the singing girls among 'forbidden pleasures'. However, the religion he founded, Islam, developed a music of its own, with chanting of the sacred Koran inside the mosques; the *muezzin*'s elaborate call to prayer, intoned from the minaret, is still a characteristic sound in every Muslim country.

There was another great period of court music-making under the Eastern Arab caliphs of the seventh and eighth centuries, culminating in the rule of Haroun al-Rashid, the central figure of the *Arabian Nights*. By the ninth century, *al-musiqi* (music) was a subject of study in Arab universities, and a number of important books, based on the musical theory of the Greeks, were produced: a classical Arab music is based on various types of *maqaam* (melody) and a set of different rhythmic modes called *iqa*, a system that recalls the Indian raga and tala.

In the West, Spain became part of Islam early in the eighth century, and music flourished under the caliphs of Cordova: the story goes that one great musician, Al-Farabi, played the lute to such effect that he could make his hearers laugh, weep, or go to sleep according to which mode he chose to play in. The remains of Arab Spain fell to Ferdinand and Isabella in 1492, but its influence on European music was considerable, through the oriental minstrels who continued to wander the continent; through the adoption of the lute and another important stringed instrument, the *rebec*; and through the Greek theory of music, which would have been lost to the Western world in the Dark Ages, had it not survived to be passed on into the mainstream of Western music through the work of the great Arab intellectuals.

And so, in this chapter, we have outlined some of the world's main musical traditions so that, when we come to trace the story of music in the West a little later on, we shall be able to think of it in a wider context. That story unfolds principally in Europe; only in its later stages does it move to the New World, unknown to Europe until the discoveries of the great transatlantic explorers. But, long before they sailed, we know that in the Americas, as in every place of human habitation, the universal language of music flourished, among the native Indian populations and in the empires of the Aztecs and the Incas.

3
Making Music

Just as no one can say with any certainty how and where music originally began, so also it is impossible to enumerate all the different instruments which are used to make music around the world. There must undoubtedly be many thousands of them, in a great variety of shapes and sizes, some strange, some beautiful, some very simple, some immensely complex, and some which in themselves are works of art.

But for all this variety, instruments can be grouped into four main classes: objects which are blown (WIND instruments), objects which produce noise through the vibration of a string (STRINGED instruments), objects which are banged or hit (PERCUSSION instruments), and the most recent addition, ELECTRICAL instruments of various kinds. In this chapter we shall refer to each of these classes in turn, together with some of the well-known music in which they appear. But first of all we must mention the most fundamental of all instruments: the human voice.

Wind Instruments

The VOICE is, of course, the original WIND instrument, since it is made to sound by a column of air produced by that natural pair of bellows, the lungs. Singers have to learn to control the breathing process with great accuracy, since the intensity of sound produced will depend on the way the column of air is directed to the *vocal cords*. These tiny membranes in the throat (only half an inch long in a full-grown man), which are wide apart as breath is taken in, come together during the act of singing or speaking and vibrate with varying degrees of tension to produce notes of higher or lower pitch. These vibrations are made audible by means of parts of the head and upper body, such as the chest cavity, the mouth and the spaces behind the nose, which vibrate in sympathy with the vocal cords and so act as *resonators*. The range of sounds produced by an individual depends on the length of the vocal chords and his or her resonating capacity, and this fact provides the basis for six major types of human voice, classified according to the range of notes they can produce: soprano, mezzo-soprano and contralto are the three main categories of female voice, in descending order of pitch, with tenor, baritone and bass as their male equivalents, though it must not be forgotten that young males often have wonderful soprano voices, and that there are adult male altos and also 'counter-tenors' whose high and brilliant register is often employed by composers.

There is, of course, an enormous range of music of all kinds for the

Sections of a modern orchestra

Percussion instruments

French horns

Harps

Violins

(from above to below) Piccolo, flutes, oboes, cor anglais, backed by bass clarinet, clarinets, bassoons and *(third row)* French horns

Trumpets backed by trombones and tuba

Cellos

Double basses

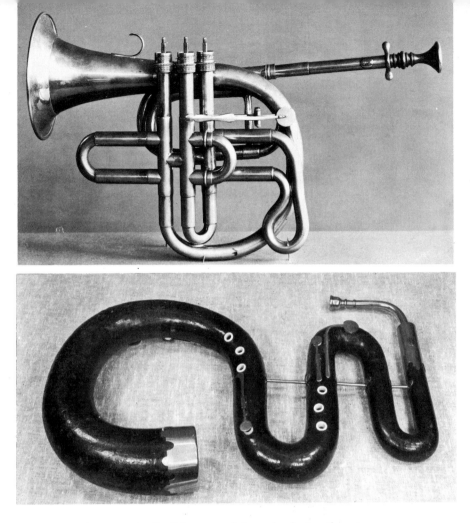

ABOVE An English cornet of the early nineteenth century.
BELOW A nineteenth-century English serpent

voice, from the expressive simplicity of folk song to that most elaborate of art forms, opera. All of us can sing to some extent, but most professional singers have to undergo a period of training, which is often long and arduous. Perfect control and 'placing' of the voice are often difficult to achieve, and the question of style, in presenting music of different types, creates many problems.

From the very origins of music, man began to invent instruments which are made to sound by human breath. In the space at our disposal we can discuss only a few of the most familiar types. First we come to WOODWIND instruments, so called because they are predominantly made of wood.

The FLUTE family is divided into two branches, depending on whether the instruments are end-blown or side-blown. The *end-blown* kind includes the six-holed TIN WHISTLE, the FLAGEOLET, the PIPE of medieval times (which had only three holes and so could be played by one person simultaneously with a small drum or tabor), and the RECORDER. The most familiar *side-blown* flute is the CONCERT FLUTE as used in most symphony orchestras: the player blows across a hole in the side of the instrument and sets the column of air inside vibrating. The flute, with a range of three octaves, is capable of great brilliance and agility. Composers frequently use it to imitate bird song; it takes the part of the Bird in *Peter and the Wolf* by Serge Prokofiev (1891–1953). Still more shrill is the PICCOLO, with a pitch an octave higher than the flute. There is also a BASS FLUTE, but this is seldom heard.

A very large group of wind instruments is sounded by means of a vibrating *reed* or reeds: among them are the OBOE and CLARINET families. Oboe-type instruments employ a *double reed* (two reeds fastened together) as a mouthpiece, fixed to the end of a conical tube. The modern orchestral oboe has many ancestors which were, in their time, extremely popular. Such was the SHAWM of the Middle Ages, and the HAUTBOY of the sixteenth and seventeenth centuries, the oboe's immediate predecessor, which derived its name from the French *hautbois* (a 'loud-toned instrument of wood'). The present-day oboe still has a very penetrating voice. It can also sound extremely poignant. But the oboe is capable of a very wide range of expression, wonderfully displayed, for example, in Mozart's Oboe Quartet. The oboe's close relatives include the COR ANGLAIS, lower in pitch than the oboe, with a bulb-shaped end, whose plaintive tones are heard to great advantage in *The Swan of Tuonela*, a tone-poem by Sibelius; the BASSOON, whose bass voice is produced from a tube doubled back on itself, and which is often used to comic effect by composers, for example as the Broomstick in *The Sorcerer's Apprentice* by Dukas; and also the DOUBLE BASSOON, which sounds an octave lower than the bassoon. It makes rare but effective appearances in a number of orchestral works, including *The Sorcerer's Apprentice*, where it appears as the lower half of the Broomstick after the Apprentice has foolishly broken it in two.

The CLARINET family employs a *single reed*, which effectively blocks off one end of a cylindrical tube: again, there is a whole range of instruments of this type, the most common being the orchestral SOPRANO CLARINETS tuned in the keys of B flat or A major. These, dating from the end of the seventeenth century, are extremely expressive instruments, and they have been frequently employed by composers in many types of music, including Mozart's great Clarinet Concerto in A major and Clarinet Quintet in the same key. Like the flute, the clarinet has a smaller brother, the SOPRANINO CLARINET, whose high tones are a regular feature of military bands, and there is a BASS CLARINET, whose shape rather resembles a saxophone. Similar in outline is the tenor BASSET HORN, now little used except in performances of older music, but at one time very popular. There is also a rarely heard ALTO CLARINET, and a CONTRABASS or double-bass clarinet which is sometimes included in European military bands.

Now we move from woodwind instruments to BRASS instruments, which are most frequently constructed of that material, though not invariably.

Brass instruments are sometimes called *lip-reeds*, for the lips of the player act rather like the double reed of the oboe family, producing different notes by means of carefully controlled vibration. This technique is extremely difficult to acquire, particularly in the case of the FRENCH HORN, which some people consider the most challenging of all instruments to play well. The orchestral horn is in fact an intricately coiled tube more than eleven feet long which widens gradually over its whole length and terminates in a large 'bell' a foot or so in diameter. The valves on the modern French horn have the effect of lengthening or shortening the tube, enabling it to obtain a full range of notes, unlike the HUNTING HORN, which can produce a few notes only, harmonically related to its natural sound. The French horn is frequently used to produce a 'hunting' effect by composers, as in the famous Rondo from Mozart's Fourth Horn Concerto; but it also has a beautiful singing quality, which can be heard in such works as the Nocturne from Mendelssohn's incidental music for *A Midsummer Night's Dream* and the slow movement of Tchaikovsky's Fifth Symphony.

There are many variants in the TRUMPET family, but they all share an essential distinction from the horns, in that the trumpet tube is not conical but retains the same dimensions throughout, except for the 'bell' at the end. Nowadays the most generally used orchestral instrument is the B FLAT TRUMPET, which consists of fifty-three inches of drawn brass tubing wound in a single loop, though teams of fanfare trumpeters often use straight instruments. Among fine trumpet concertos are those by Haydn and Hummel. The B flat trumpet has a number of near relations: there is one in D which particularly suits the high trumpet parts of the eighteenth century; and the so-called BACH TRUMPET, a long, straight instrument produced towards the end of the nineteenth century specially for Bach's music. They are little used today; and this is also true of the BASS TRUMPET, first made to Wagner's specification for his great cycle of operas *The Ring of the Nibelung*.

The bass trumpet is first cousin to the TROMBONE family of instruments, which can be fitted with valves, but much more usually are equipped with a 'slide' arrangement which enables the player to lengthen or shorten the tube and so vary the basic pitch. Trombones are descended from the SACKBUTS of former times. The one most commonly found in orchestras today is the B FLAT (or TENOR) TROMBONE, with the addition of the BASS TROMBONE. They are used to powerful effect by most major composers, and never more memorably than by Mozart (who didn't normally use them) in his opera *Don Giovanni*, when they announce the arrival at supper of an uninvited ghost. Trombones also play an essential part in most military and brass bands, as does the TUBA group of instruments.

In the Deccan, India: a musical attendant of the eighteenth century

These exist in various forms in different countries, but the one generally used in symphony orchestras is the F BASS TUBA, which supplies the bass line in the brass section. It rarely has a chance for solo display, but there is a delightful Tuba Concerto by Ralph Vaughan Williams (1872–1958). The B flat tenor tuba or EUPHONIUM is the most powerful instrument and chief tenor soloist in military and brass bands. There is also a strange European relative of the tuba called the HELICON, which is wound round the player, under one shoulder and over the other; even more spectacular is the SOUSAPHONE, introduced in the United States to the specification of the famous march-composer, John Philip Sousa (1854–1932), in which a huge detachable bell two feet in diameter stretches up above the player's head. Apart from its use in military bands, it was often included in jazz bands of the 1920s.

Among other wind instruments which are important in brass and military bands are the CORNET, a lively and agile instrument which shares characteristics of the trumpet and horn families; the B FLAT FLUGELHORN, a development of the simple military bugle with a deep funnel-shaped mouthpiece; and the SAXHORNS, a family of seven instruments ranging from deep bass to high treble invented by the Belgian Adolphe Sax (1814–1894) – these are also based on the bugle, with a conical bore like the French horn, though wider. Sax was also the inventor of the SAXOPHONE, whose family numbers twelve in all, from highest to lowest. It is a hybrid instrument, made of brass, with a flared tube like an oboe and a single reed like a clarinet. The saxophone, used in military and sometimes in brass bands, plays an important role in jazz and dance music, and sometimes appears in the symphony orchestra – in Gershwin's *Rhapsody in Blue*, for instance, and as an effective symbol of hypocritical friendship in Vaughan Williams's ballet *Job*.

Before we leave wind instruments, we must not forget the noblest and most resplendent of them all, the ORGAN or, as it's called in America, the PIPE ORGAN, to distinguish it from the electric organs which now exist in such numbers, and which we shall mention in the last section of this chapter.

The idea of making a collection of pipes sound by means of compressed air is a very ancient one which can be traced back to the second century B.C. Organ construction is a highly developed art of great complexity, but we may perhaps sum up the broad principle of the instrument thus: air is supplied to a windchest, and thence, by means of mechanical, pneumatic or electrical controls, depending on the type of organ, it is allowed to flow to the pipe or pipes required to sound. The controls are operated by the organist, sitting at the 'console', the framework carrying the keys, stops and pedals. He has one keyboard to operate with his feet, and from one to four or even five keyboards are operated manually. Above the 'manuals' (hand-keyboards) there are additional keys which, together with draw-stops fixed into panels on either side of the console, bring into operation sets of pipes of varying tone-quality – for example 'flute',

Celebes players of wooden pipes

'oboe', 'clarinet' and 'trumpet' – and introduce into the organ certain special effects such as a 'tremolo'.

The literature of organ music is very extensive; but the newcomer could do worse than listen to one or more of the many organ concertos of Handel, the great Toccata and Fugue in D minor of Bach, and – representing the spectacular nineteenth-century type of organ music – the Toccata by the French composer Charles Widor (1844–1937).

Now we must move on from wind instruments – though we have only mentioned a few of the better-known ones – to

Stringed Instruments

Again, the number and variety of such instruments around the world is immense. We shall take as our starting-point the four main stringed instruments of the symphony orchestra: the violin, viola, cello (violoncello) and double bass.

The VIOLIN family, which, on account of its eloquent tone and extreme versatility, is now probably the most important component of instrumental music, dates from the sixteenth century.

No one seems quite sure how the violin originated, but we first hear of its being used for folk music; in those early days it was certainly considered socially inferior to the VIOLS, which were used by 'people of taste' for domestic entertainment. Eventually, however, the viols were superseded by the violin family, though they are still made and used for the performance of old music.

The two types of instrument are quite distinct: viols generally have six strings, while violins have four; violin necks are smooth, as opposed to the necks of viols, which are divided by small metal 'frets', rather like guitars; the back of a viol is flat, the violin's back is convex; and while the shoulders of violin-type instruments are rounded, those of the viols have sloping shoulders, a feature which has been passed on to the one member of the violin family which is directly derived from the viols, the double bass.

The violin family are beautiful in appearance as well as tone, and astronomical prices are paid for instruments by great makers such as Nicolò Amati (1596–1684) and his pupil Antonio Stradivari (1644–1737), who both flourished with their families in the north Italian town of Cremona. Much depends on the wood chosen for the back and belly of the instrument, on its exact degree of curvature, the shape and placing of the sound holes; and the maker has to take account of the great strain imposed on the structure by the tension on the strings (about ninety-six pounds).

Violins can be plucked with the fingers in the style known as *pizzicato* as well as played with a bow, and a great many different kinds of tone can be produced by applying the bow to the string in different ways and at different distances from the 'bridge'; sometimes composers require violins to be played with the back of the bow, *col legno*, 'with the wood'.

Eighteenth-century instruments: ABOVE a German clavichord and
BELOW a French viola d'amore

Since the violin family constitutes the most prominent component of most orchestras, their qualities can be heard in most orchestral compositions. But a very much better idea of the infinite eloquence of these instruments comes from listening to them in solo compositions, or as a string quartet (two violins, viola, cello), a musical ensemble which has attracted composers to create some of the most profound and beautiful music ever written. Newcomers to such music often find the quartets of Schubert, which are melodious, deeply moving, and sometimes highly dramatic, a good starting-point. The quartets of Haydn, Mozart and Beethoven are inexhaustible treasures.

Innumerable solos have been written for the violin; among the most immediately attractive concertos for violin and orchestra are those by Beethoven, Mendelssohn, Tchaikovsky, Elgar and Sibelius. The VIOLA has been less well served as a solo instrument, but has enjoyed a revival in recent years thanks to the work of the great English virtuoso Lionel Tertis (b. 1876): there are several modern concertos for the instrument and it plays a prominent part in Berlioz's attractive *Harold in Italy*. The CELLO rivals the violin as a solo instrument of great expressiveness, and has attracted its own extensive range of music. The portrait of the Swan in *The Carnival of the Animals* by Camille Saint-Saëns (1835–1921) exploits the cello's gift for poignant melody; much more challenging to the

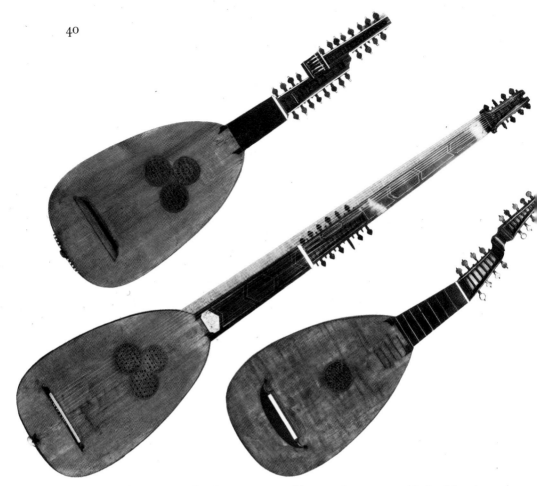

Seventeenth-century Italian instruments: a chittarone between two kinds of theorbo

listener are the unaccompanied cello suites of Bach, and glorious indeed are the cello concertos of Elgar, Dvorak and Haydn among others. Another very beautiful work which sets the violin and cello off against each other is the famous 'Double' Concerto of Brahms.

The DOUBLE BASS, like the bassoon, tends to be thought of as a gruff object of fun – that's the way it's used by Saint-Saëns in the role of the Elephant in *The Carnival of the Animals*; but there have been double-bass virtuosi, among them the famous conductor Serge Koussevitzky (1876–1951).

Apart from the violin family, one of the most popular of stringed instruments is the GUITAR. Equipped generally with six strings and with a 'fretted' finger-board which enables notes to be found more easily, it has an almost universal appeal nowadays for informal music-making: most people can easily learn to play a few chords on the instrument and so can accompany themselves or others in folk-type songs. But the guitar as used to accompany *flamenco* singing and dancing in Spain, or as a solo instrument in 'serious' music, is a very different proposition, demanding long practice and the utmost skill from the performer. Much of the present status of the guitar is due to the work and influence of the Spanish guitarist Andrés Segovia (b. 1894), who has inspired a number of brilliant virtuosi and stimulated many composers. Thus there are now a great many new works and arrangements of music for guitar to listen to: one attractive concerto which shows off the guitar in many moods is the *Concierto de Aranjuez* by Rodrigo. Among close relatives of the guitar are the MANDOLIN, descended from the LUTE family, and plucked with a plectrum instead of the fingers; either method is used for playing that lively instrument of Negro origin the BANJO, depending on whether the strings are made of gut or wire.

The HARP belongs to a very ancient line of instruments in which a number of strings are stretched over an open frame and plucked with the fingers. There are many kinds of harp, ranging from the CLARSACH of Gaelic lands and the TELYN of Wales to the DOUBLE-ACTION HARP of the modern orchestra. There it often makes a dazzling contribution through its ability to play thrilling cascades of notes. There are also large numbers of original works and arrangements for the harp.

Obviously related to the harp is the HARPSICHORD, in which a harp-type arrangement of strings is laid horizontally in a box and plucked by quills activated by the keys of a keyboard. The PIANOFORTE is, of course, also a stringed instrument in the sense that, like the harpsichord, it has a series of strings stretched over a rigid frame placed either in a horizontal box ('grand' piano) or a vertical one ('upright' piano); but in the case of the pianoforte the strings are hit by hammers instead of being plucked by quills, a fact that leads some scholars, and some composers, to classify it among percussion rather than stringed instruments.

Nowadays the keyboard repertoire tends to be played on the kind of instrument for which it was originally conceived: music of the seventeenth and eighteenth centuries is often entrusted to the harpsichord (there are many fine modern examples of the instrument) while the pianoforte or piano can concentrate on the music designed for it (broadly speaking, from the late eighteenth century onwards). The piano is music's maid-of-all-work as well as one of the finest of solo instruments, versatile enough to express anything from the poetic yearnings of Chopin or Schumann to the percussive brilliance of Béla Bartók (1881–1945).

That highly successful hybrid the pianoforte, then, can serve as a link from stringed instruments to

Percussion Instruments

These are certainly among the oldest instruments known to man, for there can be no more obvious way of producing noise, pleasant or unpleasant, than by hitting something. As with the other types of instrument, the percussion family is very large and varied: once again we concentrate on the percussion instruments most often found in our own musical tradition.

Of the many kinds of drum in general use, the most important in the symphony orchestra is the KETTLEDRUM. It consists of a large bowl of metal with a membrane, traditionally of prepared calfskin, stretched over its open end; the pitch of the drum is changed by altering the tension of this membrane. This is generally done by manually twisting a number of screws around the edge of the drum, but there are also various mechanical methods of tuning. The kettledrum performer (or 'tympanist', from the Italian word for a kettledrum) usually has three or four such drums in a modern orchestra. They are heard to fine effect at the opening of Beethoven's Violin Concerto, and make a spectacular contribution to the Requiem of Berlioz, who asks for eight pairs of drums and no fewer than ten players.

The SIDE DRUM is a small drum with a wooden shell and two sides covered in parchment. Across one side are stretched eight or ten lines of gut or silk bound together with wire which are known as 'snares'. These give the drum its characteristic rattling sound and an alternative name, SNARE DRUM. It is normally played with two wooden sticks, but in jazz and dance bands a pair of wire brushes is often used. Descended from the medieval TABOR, the side drum is particularly effective in a military context. It is very difficult to learn to play 'rolls' on the instrument, but once mastered they contribute a great sense of anticipation and excitement.

Another regular member of the symphony orchestra is the BASS DRUM, a large drum with a wooden shell whose membranes or 'drumheads' are usually some thirty-two inches in diameter. It is played with a stick with a large felt head. Generally the bass drum is mounted on its side, but sometimes it is laid flat to produce an even more thunderous effect: one of the most dramatic appearances of this big drum is in the *Dies Irae* ('Day of Wrath') movement from Verdi's Requiem.

The TAMBOURINE is a much smaller member of the drum family, with an ancient lineage dating from Biblical times. Nowadays it has a membrane on only one side, and circular metal jingles are inserted into the wooden frame. Its orchestral appearances are frequent, and it has come to have a special association with the street-corner evangelism of the Salvation Army. TOMTOMS derived from African native drums were introduced into jazz bands in the 1920s and are still part of many jazz drum-kits.

Turning to other types of percussion instruments used in the orchestra, a set of TUBULAR BELLS is often found: their appearance in Tchaikovsky's famous '1812' Overture, when they represent the bells of Moscow, comes instantly to mind. The GLOCKENSPIEL, a set of steel plates mounted on a stand and played with two little hammers, gives a bell-like tone of great delicacy. Even more ethereal is the CELESTE, a small keyboard instrument with wooden resonators under its steel plates: perhaps its most famous appearance is in the Dance of the Sugar Plum Fairy from Tchaikovsky's 'Nutcracker' Ballet. The XYLOPHONE, a graduated series of wooden bars played with two beaters, is quite often used in orchestral scores (one recalls the amusing impersonation of the Fossils in *The Carnival of the Animals* by Saint-Saëns), and it is also a source of entertainment as a virtuoso solo instrument.

The TRIANGLE is a small steel bar bent into a figure of three sides and played with a small metal rod. Its high, bell-like sound is in sharp contrast to the crash of the CYMBALS – large circular brass plates which can be fitted with leather handles and clashed together using both hands; or they can be attached to big drums in some military and jazz drum-kits. Cymbals can also be 'rolled' in a hushed or menacing way. The large

An English nineteenth-century tabor, and a modern workshop for radiophonic instruments

gong, or TAMTAM, struck with a soft drumstick, can be used to great effect in creating an oriental atmosphere, while the CASTANETS (two small hollow pieces of wood clashed together in the hand or, in the orchestra, attached to a stick and shaken) are indispensable in creating a Spanish or Latin American sound. An orchestral ANVIL is sometimes required, as in Josef Strauss's *Feuerfest* Polka and the Anvil Chorus in Verdi's opera *Il Trovatore*; and in modern music an ever-growing variety of percussion instruments of more unconventional kinds is demanded, ranging from RATTLES, BLOCKS and WHIPS to TYPEWRITERS and IRON CHAINS.

Nowadays, apart from the long-established wind, string and percussion families of instruments, musicians can make use of a growing number of

Electrical Instruments

Indeed, it is difficult to think how that staple combination of modern 'pop' music, the 'group', could exist without them. In the ELECTRIC GUITARS so often used by 'pop' musicians, the sound from the vibrating wires of the instrument is used to set up an electro-magnetic current which is fed through an amplifier to a loudspeaker. The ELECTRIC (or ELECTROPHONIC) ORGAN works rather differently, for here the sound is actually created by electrical oscillations which are converted into audible form and amplified. Through analysis of the acoustic components of sounds produced by other instruments, the pattern of oscillation can be made to imitate these sounds, and the quality of the best electric organs, sometimes operated in conjunction with a computer which 'remembers' the tones produced by fine pipe organs, can be very satisfying. On a less ambitious scale, the absence of pipes has made it possible for such makes of electric organ as the Hammond and the Compton to be installed in many homes, and their compactness and competitive price, coupled with increasingly 'authentic' sound, has won them acceptance in many public settings. A great many other effects in addition to traditional organ sound were added to the THEATRE ORGANS so often built for super-cinemas and theatres in the twenties and thirties: bird calls, train whistles, motor horns and a variety of crashes and bangs were often introduced to help in providing a sound track for silent films or giving novelty to a solo organ 'spot'.

Nowadays the science of electronics is such that computers can be programmed to compose music, and synthesizers can reproduce with uncanny realism the sound of almost any instrument, even the human voice: some modern composers make use of such devices together with more traditional instruments, combining the two in performance with the help of the TAPE RECORDER. This is one of a further group of electrical instruments used in the reproduction rather than the creation of music. Its elder brothers, the RADIO and the GRAMOPHONE, have played an incredibly influential role on the musical scene of the twentieth century, making music of a high standard easily available to everyone.

Sixteenth-century crumhorns, recently brought back to use.
OVERLEAF An angel trumpeter from a thirteenth-century manuscript

4
The Written Language of Music

All of us at some time or another have heard a tune we like and had the embarrassing experience of trying to tell someone else how it goes. Unless we happen to have a good musical memory and the ability to sing in tune, we shall probably make a more or less clumsy attempt to hum or whistle the tune, accompanied perhaps by a vague 'oom-pah-pah' here and there to suggest the rhythm. Quite obviously such a method of transmitting music from one person to another leaves much to be desired; and yet a great deal of the world's most beautiful music – folk songs and the like – has been passed down in just this way from generation to generation. Very often, of course, folk musicians are accomplished and skilful, so their efforts at teaching others would be far more accurate than those of the untutored amateur; but many well-known folk songs have been considerably modified during their passage through the years, and a number can be found in different forms in different places. Thus there is a rich and living diversity in folk music which might not have developed if the original notes had been written down generations ago; but who knows how many songs have been lost for ever? Only in comparatively recent times, when easy travel and mass entertainment tend to threaten local individuality, have musical scholars set out to collect and note down folk songs, before they vanish, from those old enough to remember them.

Such scholars now have at their disposal established methods of writing music down, but such methods had to be invented; and even then they were often inadequate and ambiguous. Imagine for a moment that no established way of writing music down exists and that instead of trying to hum a tune to your friend, you are going to *draw* the melody. Well, you might achieve a line which goes up and down more or less as the tune does; but how do you show how long each note lasts, on which note the tune begins, how loud or soft it should be, whether it swings along like a march or sways like a waltz (the rhythm of the tune)? All this information and much more besides must be communicated to the reader if a written musical language is to convey anything like the reality it represents.

The need for such a code was felt in the earliest days of recorded civilization. Music created for religious and court ceremonies, according to rules which often had the force of holy writ, and often involving large numbers of performers, clearly called for some definite, authoritative means of transmission. We know, for instance, that a different written symbol expressed each of the five notes of the traditional Chinese scale more than a thousand years before the birth of Christ, and that around

ABOVE A *dhambiro*-player at a wedding in Pakistan.
BELOW Guatemalan boys playing a xylophone

Notation in the tenth and
RIGHT the sixteenth century

700 B.C. a series of two hundred and ninety-seven symbols were used in India to represent the subtle vocal inflections required in performing the Vedic hymns. Systems of musical notation also existed in the ancient empires of Babylonia and Egypt.

The letters of the alphabet were used to distinguish different notes in the instrumental music of ancient Greece – an idea that passed into Arab musical theory on the one hand, and into Europe on the other, for we find alphabetical symbols describing musical notes in documents surviving from the third century of the Christian era, together with a number of signs of timing and phrasing which have survived, with modifications, into our own times. For example:

⌒ binding two or three notes together
— above a note, lengthening it
⌢ representing a pause; it is now written ⌒

We owe the development of our own sophisticated system of musical notation to the desire of the early Church to standardize and pass on its method of intoning psalms and prayers. This style of unaccompanied singing, derived from Hebrew and Greek influences, is known as PLAINSONG (or PLAINCHANT), and very eloquent it can be.

A very large body of such music rapidly grew up in early Christian times, and two major attempts were made to set it in order, the first by St Ambrose, Bishop of Milan (c. A.D. 340–397), and the second under Pope Gregory the Great (c. A.D. 540–604). They were able to make use of alphabetical notation and of a set of signs known as NEUMES, which gave a somewhat inexact indication of the way a particular chant moved up and down, but at least served as a reminder to the singer of the shape of a tune.

The earliest neumes merely consisted of a series of dots and curves together with signs resembling our grave, acute and circumflex accents, written on and around a single horizontal line: a system of neume notation is still used for plainsong in the Church, but it now gives precise indications, and the signs are arranged on a grid, STAVE or STAFF of four lines.

Other music is now written on a stave of five lines.

The idea of arranging note-symbols on and between a set of equally-spaced lines is credited to a remarkable Benedictine monk called Guido of Arezzo (b. c. A.D. 995), who seems to have put together most of the basic thoughts behind our present-day systems of notations. He used coloured lines to indicate certain notes – red for F and yellow for C – or marked the lines representing these notes with the signs or CLEFS

         (for F)   and   (for C)

which are still used today; though in modern music the C, or *alto*, clef is rarely used except for viola parts, and we are now accustomed to see our music written on the G or treble stave or clef

coupled with the F or bass clef

Once the positions of these notes on the stave have been established, then the remainder of the notes in our scale, named according to the letters of the alphabet from A to G, can be placed on the other lines or spaces of the stave. The alphabetical sequence repeats itself at the eighth note (the 'octave'). Thus, using two staves for the treble and bass clef, plus a few extra 'ledger' lines at the top and bottom and in between, we can represent a very large range of notes.

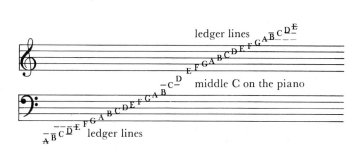

So much for our system of placing notes according to their PITCH. What of the duration of each note? Again, it was in the early Middle Ages that different shapes of note began to be used to indicate differing

Manuscript of keyboard music by
Johann Sebastian Bach and
BELOW RIGHT of an opera score
by Richard Wagner

durations, and by degrees they became recognizable as the ones we use today. These are some of the more common, together with their British and American names:

	British	American
𝅝	semi-breve	whole note
𝅗𝅥	minim	half note
𝅘𝅥	crotchet	quarter note
𝅘𝅥𝅮	quaver	eighth note
𝅘𝅥𝅯	semi-quaver	sixteenth note

Now, with the ability to place a note in pitch and indicate its duration, we can begin to think of writing down the line of a melody. But what of its rhythm? In medieval Church music, vertical lines were sometimes drawn, to indicate how the various parts in choral singing fitted together; later these became 'bar lines', used to divide the music into sections, called BARS or MEASURES, of equal time-value, and which generally imply a certain amount of accent or stress on the first note of each bar. In the latter part of the seventeenth century the time-value of each bar in a piece of music was further defined by the introduction of a TIME SIGNATURE, placed after the clef-sign at the beginning of a composition. The time signature contains two numbers, the upper one representing the number of units in each bar, and the lower one the value or duration of those units. For example $\frac{3}{4}$ means three crotchets, or quarter notes, to each bar. This is, among other things, the rhythm of the waltz. The signature $\frac{4}{4}$ means four crotchets to a bar, and this is often the time of a march.

In modern written music, there is a further 'signature' to look for at the beginning of a composition. This is the KEY SIGNATURE, and to explain this we must once again go back to our medieval Churchmen who inherited most of their musical ideas from classical Greece.

Greek musical theory established sequences, or SCALES, of notes arranged in seven patterns or MODES. The intervals between individual notes varied in the different modes, each of which was thought to produce a different emotional effect. In his fourth-century review of Church music, St Ambrose reduced the number of modes to four, known as the 'authentic' modes: Pope Gregory increased them by the addition of four 'plagal' modes, and a Swiss monk called Glareanus added another four in the sixteenth century. This 'modal' system gives early music a special and, some think, a specially attractive colour, and a number of later composers have returned to it.

Of the twelve modes as understood by Glareanus, two (the so-called Ionian and Aeolian) survived to give us our system of MAJOR and MINOR KEYS, a 'key' being a related system of notes based on a particular note; and these two keys, together with the harmonic relationships between them, provided the basic material of musical composition for

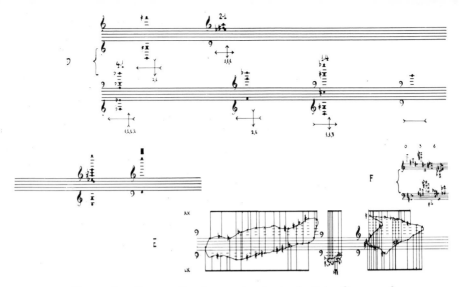

Manuscript of a score for piano and orchestra by John Cage, 1958

three centuries. Since 1900, however, among *avante-garde* (experimental) composers there has been a widespread reaction against the key or 'tonal' system. Much modern music is ATONAL (that is, not tonal) and based on new kinds of musical scale.

However, in tonal music, which means most familiar music, the intervals between the notes of a major key are always the same, no matter on what note the scale begins; there are two types of minor scale, but again the intervals of these scales are consistently the same, no matter on which note the scale begins.

If you look at the keyboard of that most familiar of instruments, the pianoforte, you will see that it consists of a series of white and black keys. The musical intervals between immediately consecutive notes (that is, between a white and black note where they lie together and between two whites when they are adjacent) is called a SEMITONE, representing half a TONE; and a scale completely consisting of semitones – that is, every note on the piano taken in strict succession – is called a CHROMATIC SCALE. The MAJOR and MINOR SCALES (known together as DIATONIC SCALES) each use a selection of notes from the chromatic scale arranged, in the case of the major scale, to represent the following intervals between its eight notes:

1	whole tone
2	whole tone
3	semitone (half a whole tone)
4	whole tone
5	whole tone
6	whole tone
7	semitone (half a whole tone)

Minor scales also have unalterable interval patterns.

Depending on the first note, or KEYNOTE, chosen for the scale, certain notes in the scale will need to be 'sharpened' (raised a semitone), using the sign ♯, or 'flattened' (lowered a semitone), using the sign ♭, to produce the required sequence of intervals, and it is this requirement which gives rise to the key signature of a piece of music. The keys of C major and A minor require no SHARPS or FLATS; but the key of G requires that the note F should be sharpened. This would be indicated at the start of a piece thus:

or

while the key of F requires that the note B should be flattened, indicated thus:

Other keys require more sharps or flats. For example E flat major and C minor require three flats:

or

F major and C sharp minor require four sharps:

or

So, with a little practice, when you look at a page of music you can tell the pitch of the notes (from the clef sign), the key (from the key-signature) and the rhythm (from the time-signature). The shapes of the notes will tell you their relative duration, the bar lines where the accent falls. From the late seventeenth century onwards, composers began adding indications of speed and expression at the head of their manuscripts or 'scores' (these are often in Italian but the vocabulary can soon be mastered – for example *allegro* means lively and *andante* means 'at a walking pace'), and in 1816 a machine called the metronome was invented which enabled composers for the first time to give precise indications of the speed at which they wanted their compositions played. The indication '♩ = 6o' would mean sixty crotchets or quarter notes to the minute, and the performer's metronome could be set to beat out this time.

This book is no place to go further into the technique of reading and writing music, and a course of study is the only way to learn about the subject properly. But for the very young, and for others who find it unnecessary to master the intricacies of STAFF NOTATION, another system exists.

This is TONIC SOL-FA. It gives the following names to the notes of the major scale: Doh, Ray, Me, Fah, Soh, Lah, Te, Doh (with variations for minor keys). The system as we know it came into use in the nineteenth century, but for the original idea behind tonic sol-fa we are again indebted to that brilliant Benedictine, Guido of Arezzo. He divided the notes within a choir's compass into 'hexachords', scales of six notes which he named Ut, Re, Mi, Fa, Sol and La, terms borrowed, so it's said, from an eighth-century hymn by Paul Diaconus (Paul 'the Deacon') to St John the Baptist:

UT queant laxis,	UTtered be thy wondrous story,
REsonare fibris,	REprehensive though I be,
MIra gestorum	ME make mindful of thy glory,
FAmuli tuorum,	FAmous son of Zacharee;
Solve polluti	Solace to my spirit bring,
LAbii reatum,	LAbouring thy praise to sing,
Sancte Johannes,	Saint John.

(Freely translated in the nineteenth century by the Rev. Ebenezer Cobham Brewer.)

In the seventeenth century, the unsingable Ut had become Doh, and the seventh or 'leading' note had been added to the scale and called Te.

Before we end this chapter it should perhaps be said that, for all the sophistication of our present methods of writing music down, there are those who think them increasingly inadequate – for example, in representing the microtones which occur in oriental, and more recently in electronic, music. A number of modern composers, eager to free themselves from all the conventional trappings of music, have had to devise novel patterns of notation to match; but for the majority of us staff notation and tonic sol-fa are still valid tools.

Whatever system is used, it takes time and practice to learn to read music fluently, just as it does to play an instrument. It is well worth doing, even if you are not a great performer, for then you can gain a better understanding of fine music. Even so, it is important to remember that the music you can read from a page of paper is no more than the circuit diagram is to the television set. Television sets do not light up without the craft of the engineer, nor will music live without the talent of the interpretive artist, who must be able to sense a composer's real intention through the medium of the written code.

5
Some Shapes of Music

Just as performers of music around the world have at their disposal an almost limitless array of instruments, so we find that music itself is fashioned into countless shapes.

Chaos is not a condition human beings enjoy; and one of the prime objects of art through the ages has been to create a satisfying pattern out of the apparently chaotic conditions which surround us. There have been endless arguments about the nature of such a pattern, and there is, at the present time, a school of thought in music as in the other arts which seeks to abandon the idea of pattern or shape altogether. This approach emphasizes spontaneity at the expense of almost every other consideration; and although spontaneity is a desirable human trait, it is doubtful if exciting new music can often emerge when the hundred or so players in an orchestra are directed to play as and when the fancy seizes them. Some 'composers' go further, and would remove the element of human will altogether, as far as possible allowing music to be created through a series of accidental 'happenings'. They may be compared to the artist who believes in applying paint to the canvas by standing well back and letting fly with a full brush.

In recent years the whole concept of Order has been brought into question, and to that extent perhaps the trend of our times is essentially different from that prevailing in earlier revolutionary movements in history, which intended to abolish the old order, but only with the aim of establishing a new one. However, such is the human desire for a pattern in things, that we simply cannot be content with aimless destruction; and the struggle continues to find new, more valid ways of ordering our lives.

A number of major twentieth-century composers have broken away from the time-honoured KEY (or TONAL) system. Debussy (see page 137) and others have sometimes made use of the so-called WHOLE-TONE SCALE – that is, a scale without semitones; while Arnold Schoenberg (see page 140) established a whole new harmonic philosophy which has been widely followed. This is based on the TWELVE-TONE or CHROMATIC SCALE, and exponents of this system base their compositions on TONE-ROWS consisting of a number of notes selected from the twelve-tone scale. The effect is often discordant, but is far from formless – in fact, orthodox twelve-tone compositions are governed by strict rules; and once the listener has become accustomed to the sound and style of such compositions, many of them stand revealed as works of beauty which perhaps could not have been conceived in other terms.

Pythagoras and his disciples employing the musical scale

However, for the majority of listeners, most of the music they hear probably belongs to, or is written in the style of, the three centuries between about 1600 and about 1900 when, unchallenged, the tonal system, with its array of interrelated major and minor keys, provided the framework of music. We shall now consider briefly some of the forms of music supported by this framework. Our aim is to introduce complex questions in simple terms, advising those who wish to go further to look elsewhere. Some useful paths to pursue are recommended at the end of this volume.

Generalizations are always dangerous, but it is at least possible to argue that art satisfies our desire to perceive a pattern through the balancing principles of *repetition* and *contrast*. The symmetry we observe in the composition of a great painting or a fine piece of architecture is a kind of repetition; but this would become tiresome if it were not relieved with contrasts of shape or colour. Translated into terms of sound, the notion can be applied to music.

To find an example of repetition and contrast in music, we need go no further than any one of thousands of popular songs, which 'catch on' through constant repetition of a 'chorus' (the pleasure of recognition gives us an agreeably secure feeling), while the element of contrast may be supplied by the 'verse' which initially acts as a build-up for the chorus and later on provides relaxing interludes; or by the so-called 'middle eight' (bars) in many a pop song:

Verse   You think you've lost your love –
                Well, I saw her yesterda-a-ay.
                It's you she's thinking of,
                And she told me what to sa-a-ay.

Chorus   She says she loves you,
                And you know that can't be bad.
                She loves you,
                And you know you should be glad.
                She loves you, yeah, yeah, yeah.
                She loves you, yeah, yeah, yeah.
                She loves you, yeah, yeah, yeah, yeah.

She Loves You, 1962, Lennon and McCartney

Dr Percy Scholes, whose *Concise Oxford Dictionary of Music* is both erudite and entertaining, asserts that all musical compositions, however complicated, are constructed from no more than six kinds of musical shape. Before enumerating them, we must say a little more about the key system.

The chosen key of a particular piece of music is like base camp to the mountaineer: from it he ventures out to the unknown; to it he returns with relief once the expedition is over. By the process known as MODULATION a composer can proceed in steps (though for special effects these steps are sometimes omitted) from one given key to any other; but he can go by a direct route to certain special keys. These are the keys built on the fifth note of the major scale – the so-called DOMINANT – and the fourth note, the SUBDOMINANT.

It is also easy to move from a major key into its RELATIVE MINOR (the minor key with which it shares the same key-signature), or the other way round.

Thus if a piece of music is in the key of C major, it will very likely move away at some point into the dominant key of G major, the subdominant key of F major, or the relative minor key of A minor, before coming home, at the end of the composition, to C major again.

A young pianist or guitarist who wishes to be able to accompany himself or others in simple songs will quickly be able to do so if he chooses as a starting point the key of C major and masters four COMMON CHORDS: the one built on the TONIC keynote C (consisting of C, E, G), those built on the dominant, G (G, B, D), the subdominant, F (F, A, C), and the MINOR COMMON CHORD of the relative minor key, built on A (A, C, E). In fact, for a great many popular tunes, three chords – the tonic, dominant and subdominant – will suffice.

Having thus ventured into the fringes of harmony, we can now return to Dr Scholes's six categories of musical form.

First is the two-part form known as SIMPLE BINARY. Typically, pieces in this form begin in the main, tonic key and end their first section in the dominant. The second section leads back to a conclusion in the tonic. The structure can be seen in essentials in the four-bar chorus of Arne's 'Rule Britannia'

tonic G major   dominant   tonic G major
    chord   D major chord   chord

and it often formed the basis of extended compositions in the seventeenth and early eighteenth centuries.

Second comes a three-part form known as TERNARY form. This is very common, especially in songs and short compositions, and consists of an opening section in the tonic key, a second section in a different style or key or both, often the dominant, and a third section which substantially repeats the material of the first. An example is the song 'Cherry Ripe', which begins in C major

Cher-ry ripe, cher-ry ripe, ripe,   I   cry . . .

has a middle section effectively in the dominant G major

If   so   be   you ask me   where . . .

and returns to C major for the final section.

The third of Dr Scholes's six forms is known as COMPOUND BINARY, otherwise called SONATA form. It plays a most important role in serious music, as we shall see. In essentials it consists of Section 1 ('exposition'), in which two contrasted musical ideas are stated, the first in the tonic key and the second, typically, in the dominant or subdominant; and Section 2 ('development' and 'recapitulation'), where one or both of the principal ideas of the exposition are discussed and elaborated, and then finally restated, perhaps in modified form, to bring the piece to an end. Sonata form was first fully deployed by C.P.E. Bach (1714–1788, one of the sons of Johann Sebastian Bach, for whom see page 108) in the eighteenth century, was brought to perfection by Haydn, Mozart and Beethoven and has continued to be of great significance ever since.

Category four is the RONDO, a form comparable to ternary in that it is built up of alternate contrasting sections. But instead of the simple A, B, A of ternary form we now have something like A, B, A, C, A, D, A, in which A is the main tune and B, C and D are subsidiary episodes introduced to give variety. The rondo is one of the most frequently used of all musical forms.

The AIR WITH VARIATIONS is the fifth category defined by Dr Scholes. It is found in every kind of composition, serious and light-hearted, and consists essentially of the statement of a simple tune, which then forms the basis of a sequence of variants on the original. Sometimes the tune is repeated throughout, with the addition of decorative material or changes of speed; but, in some other compositions, only the harmonic structure of the theme is retained and the variations are varied indeed. One example of a great orchestral work in this form is the 'Enigma' Variations of Elgar (see page 141) – the composer has kept everyone guessing ever since he wrote the piece by suggesting that its true theme is never actually stated at all. Much less enigmatic but no less ingenious is the procedure commonly used in jazz, where a well-known tune is stated, followed by improvised variations on it from the various members of the band.

The sixth and last category is FUGUE form. Many kinds of composition make use of COUNTERPOINT (that is, the blending and interweaving of two or more melodic lines in a piece), but fugues use counterpoint in a special way. Firstly, in fugues, the number of melodic lines (or 'voices') is defined – for example, 'Fugue in Four Voices' – and, secondly, the fugue is built up from a SUBJECT (and possibly a COUNTER-SUBJECT) stated first by one 'voice' and then echoed by the others. A CANON such as 'Three Blind Mice' is an embryonic fugue; but the form as elaborated, for instance, by Johann Sebastian Bach becomes a mighty intellectual exercise which can also generate much emotional heat: the very well known Prelude and Fugue in D minor is but one of many examples.

Sometimes a piece of music will be quite clearly cast in one or other of these six kinds of musical shape, but often elements of more than one will be employed by a composer. Whatever kind of work is under consideration, the foregoing may perhaps serve as a set of basic clues for the would-be musical detective who wishes to discover a little more about the building-bricks of music; and we can now go on to discuss some of the more familiar large-scale musical structures.

To some people the very word SONATA strikes a forbidding note. But it simply means 'sounded' and was introduced in the seventeenth century to distinguish instrumental music from a composition for voices, to which another Italian word CANTATA ('sung') was often applied. In those days, two kinds of sonata were recognized: the SONATA DA CHIESA ('church sonata', of suitably reverential character) and the SONATA DA CAMERA ('chamber' or 'room' sonata). Both were usually written for a body of stringed instruments with keyboard accompaniment.

The sonata da camera consisted of a sequence of short pieces similar to the SUITE, a form much employed by Bach, Handel and their contemporaries. But whereas the suite was often a succession of dance rhythms – allemande, courante, sarabande, minuet, gigue, and the rest, with individual pieces frequently assuming simple binary form – the sonata began to develop a more abstract character. Domenico Scarlatti (1685–1757, an almost exact contemporary of Bach and Handel) wrote some five hundred sonatas, each usually in a single MOVEMENT; but, in the course of the eighteenth century, the sonata took on the form in which it is now most usually found, a work in four separate movements (that is, sections moving at contrasting speeds).

It was at this period, starting with C. P. E. Bach, that the first movements of sonatas began to be written in compound binary or sonata form, generally for single instruments, or a pair of instruments (violin and harpsichord, cello and piano, and other combinations). Thereafter the process of development inherent in sonata form tended to become more and more elaborate, with the result that sonata first movements generally bear most of the argumentative weight of the work as a whole. Characteristically, first movements are quick in TEMPO (speed).

Second movements are usually slow and lyrical. They are often constructed in ternary form, with a melody stated at the beginning of the movement and repeated at the end, and a contrasting middle section; but second movement form is very variable. It is the third movement which most clearly betrays the descent of the sonata from the dance suite, since very often it assumes the form of a minuet and trio, with the trio as the filling in another ternary sandwich. The fourth movement is generally fast and often light-hearted. It is here that rondo form is very frequently found, and a foot-tapping rhythm is employed to send everyone away happy.

Such is the characteristic shape of the classical sonata, a shape which underwent many variations in the masterly hands of Haydn and Mozart, and which was wrought by Beethoven into a titanic medium of expression which could encompass all the heights and depths of human emotion. Beethoven's thirty-two piano sonatas range from lucidly constructed pieces more or less in the conventional manner of the day to lengthy epics such as the 'Appassionata', 'Waldstein' and 'Hammerklavier' sonatas which exploit the dramatic possibilities of sonata form to the utmost. It is probably this dramatic potential derived from matching one musical idea against another which has made sonata form so widespread in serious music: many instrumental trios, quartets, quintets and so forth are simply sonatas for more than two instruments, and the SYMPHONY is a sonata writ large.

'Symphony' (the word is Greek in origin) means 'sounding together'. It is used in the United States to describe a large body of musicians without the addition of the word 'orchestra' – a practice which can claim the blessing of no less an authority than the poet John Milton, who speaks of the musical forces of heaven as the 'angelic symphony'. Throughout the English-speaking world, the word is applied to a major work for orchestra in sonata form (or some variant of it). 'Symphony' began to acquire this meaning at the period which saw the development of the sonata; formerly it had been applied to an instrumental interlude (for example in Handel's *Messiah*) or to what we would now call the overture or PRELUDE to a theatrical work.

Since Beethoven's day, the symphony has been thought of as perhaps the most monumental structure in music, and it is only in recent times that composers have questioned its supremacy as the ultimate in musical achievement. The one hundred and four symphonies of Haydn (usually considered the 'father' of the symphony), and the forty-one of Mozart, had already brought the art of symphonic writing to perfection when Beethoven came along. In his nine symphonies, Beethoven treated form with increasing freedom, replacing the minuet and trio, for instance, with a SCHERZO and trio. *Scherzo* is Italian for 'joke'; but although Beethoven's scherzos do sometimes provide an element of light relief after a profound slow movement, they are often made to bear considerable weight in the structure of the work as a whole (the Seventh Symphony is an example) and the 'joke' often has a serious point. In the Ninth Symphony, Beethoven makes the scherzo his second movement and, as though he felt that no conventional vehicle could possibly carry his message of brother-hood to mankind, he took the revolutionary step of breaking out in the fourth movement into an ecstatic choral finale, a setting of Schiller's *Ode to Joy*.

Other symphonic composers followed Beethoven in this as in other respects, notably Mahler (see page 139), who in his Eighth Symphony (the 'Symphony of a Thousand') carried the choral approach to the ultimate. All the major nineteenth-century symphonic composers were influenced by Beethoven, even Hector Berlioz (1803–1869), who gave the symphony new and fantastic forms, and Jean Sibelius (1865–1957), who largely redefined symphonic structure.

That other staple ingredient of concert-hall fare, the CONCERTO, is generally to be found in three movements, and is rather less portentous than the symphony, though it shares many of the characteristics of sonata form. *Concerto* is another Italian word, which signifies 'playing together', and it was applied in the seventeenth and early eighteenth centuries to a particular kind of church or chamber sonata in which a small group of solo instruments (the *concertino* or *concertante* group) was set

against the full (*ripieno*) body of players. Such was the form of the
CONCERTO GROSSO as understood by Corelli and Handel, and as
employed by Bach in three of his 'Brandenburg' concertos. But at the
same time, works for single solo instruments and orchestra were also
being written, and the term 'concerto' was applied to them too: since the
mid-eighteenth century the word has generally been used in this way.
There are a few nineteenth-century concertos for more than one solo
instrument, but in general they feature a single soloist whose part often
provides great opportunities for virtuoso display, including one or more
CADENZAS, in which the soloist, without accompaniment, produces
elaborate embroidery on the themes of the work. In the greatest concertos,
display is not allowed to obscure the musical argument as a whole, which
acquires a special 'concerto character' through the interplay or dialogue
between soloist and orchestra.

In the twentieth century, a number of composers have used the word
'concerto' once again in its older sense. An example is the brilliant
Concerto for Orchestra of Béla Bartók (1881–1945), which shows off
different sections of the orchestra in turn against the general texture of
the ensemble as a whole.

Enlightened concert promoters nowadays try to formulate new
programme plans (as is the case, for instance, with the Henry Wood
Promenade Concerts in London, under the B.B.C.'s management), but
many concerts are still to be found which follow the conventional practice
of including a symphony and a concerto and beginning the programme
with an OVERTURE. The beginning is the right place for an overture,
since it is related to the French word *ouverture*, 'opening'. Early French and
Italian operas sometimes had three-movement overtures which were in
some respects the forerunners of the symphony and were often given the
Italian name SINFONIA. As time went on, composers adopted the practice
of including, in the overtures to stage works, musical foretastes of what
was to come; often they were cast in sonata form, and so resembled
symphonic first movements. Perhaps because it was good advertising, the
practice grew up of including theatre overtures in concert programmes,
and subsequently a new kind of overture, the CONCERT OVERTURE,
was developed. This is essentially a one-movement symphony, of which
Mendelssohn's *Fingal's Cave* is a good example, and Tchaikovsky's
'1812' Overture is one of the best known. Closely related to concert
overtures are SYMPHONIC POEMS, one-movement works in more or less
symphonic form which, unlike most symphonies, often have a story to tell
and so come into the category of what is called 'programme' music. Franz
Liszt (1811–1886), Bedřich Smetana (1824–1884) and Antonin
Dvořák (see page 126) are among the many composers who wrote
symphonic poems. One of the most immediately attractive is *Till
Eulenspiegel* by Richard Strauss (1864–1949), with its vivid portrait of a
medieval rogue.

The fact that a piece of music tells a story does not of itself make it musically either 'good' or 'bad', though there are some who think 'programme' music generally is to be deplored. Such people do not belong to the great majority, who respond to a story well told, whether it is expressed in musical terms or not; and who, all through the ages, have flocked to the theatre to watch stories told in dramatic form.

In the sixth century B.C., classical Greek tragedy began to develop from dramas sung and danced by a chorus in the part of the arena which became known as the 'orchestra' of the Greek theatre, and music is known to have played a major part in the works of great tragedians such as Aeschylus. Music and mime figured largely in the 'miracle' plays of the Middle Ages which attracted great crowds around street stages, and at the same time played a major part in the masques and other diversions which entertained the noble and rich in their palaces; but it was not until the early seventeenth century that we see the beginnings of OPERA and BALLET, forms of entertainment which have produced some of the most attractive and important of all musical compositions. Like 'sonata' and 'symphony', the word 'opera' has acquired a grandeur which it did not originally possess; it grew in status on its way through the Italian language, but its humble source was the Latin word OPUS, which means 'a piece of work'. In its direct descent it still means this; indeed, most composers make use of the word to number their 'pieces of work' Opus 1, Opus 2 and so on, though you will notice that in some cases other kinds of numbering are employed. Mozart's works were catalogued by one Köchel, so the numbers are preceded by the letter K; Alessandro Longo performed the same service for Domenico Scarlatti, so Scarlatti pieces have L numbers, and works by Schubert may have both opus numbers and D numbers, the D standing for the Schubert scholar Otto Deutsch.

Opera – which we may define as drama set entirely, or almost entirely, to music – originated in Italy in 1597, with the production at Florence of Peri's *La Dafne*; later it became established with acclaim in France, Austria, Germany and other European countries. But although the operas of Handel and his rivals packed the theatres of London in the eighteenth century, and there were several successful British opera composers then and later, the idea of opera always seems to have encountered some resistance from the Anglo-Saxon public in general, who were more ready to laugh at operatic parodies such as John Gay's *The Beggar's Opera* of 1728, and the light operas of Gilbert and Sullivan in the 1870s and 1880s, than they were to enjoy the real thing. It has to be admitted that opera in the past has often been something of a gift for the parodist, because many an operatic plot is far-fetched to the point of absurdity, and the portly contours of middle-aged opera stars have often rendered them visually unsuitable for such roles as the Consumptive Heroine and the Lithe Young Hero. Fortunately for us, things have changed in the operatic world in recent years. A number of twentieth-century composers, such as

Benjamin Britten (b. 1913), Michael Tippett (b. 1905), Arthur Bliss (b. 1891), William Walton (b. 1902), George Gershwin (1898–1937) and Leonard Bernstein (b. 1918), among others, have written fine operas in English. This means that as much attention is now paid to the dramatic effectiveness of an opera as to its musical standards, and the days are over when star singers – much though they were loved for their glorious voices – travelled the world with their own costumes and their own predetermined ideas on stage movements, and would perform their favourite roles with little rehearsal and no regard for the ensemble as a whole.

The would-be opera composer has many problems, not the least of which is finding a collaborator who understands those problems. He must be capable of creating a play or 'libretto' (booklet of words) which the composer can set to music, and which works in dramatic terms. An inadequate plot has been the downfall of many an opera with fine music, while many another has survived, like Mozart's *Don Giovanni* (1787), in spite of its libretto. However, there have been some notably successful partnerships, such as the one between Giuseppe Verdi and Arrigo Boito which produced Verdi's Shakespearean masterpieces *Othello* (1887) and *Falstaff* (1893), and the collaboration of Richard Strauss with Hugo von Hofmannsthal which resulted in a number of fine works, among them one of the most romantic and appealing of all operas, *Der Rosenkavalier* ('The Rose-Cavalier'). In the field of light opera, too, there are examples of similarly happy arrangements, of which the association between Arthur Sullivan (1842–1900) and W. S. Gilbert (1836–1911) is probably the most celebrated.

Operatic composers who were unable to find suitable literary collaborators either suffered failure in the theatre (as did Schubert) or turned to writing their own stories. The most notable of such men was unquestionably Richard Wagner (see page 129), who preferred to call his great stage works 'music-dramas' rather than operas, and set out to create psychologically convincing characters, whether on the human level (as in his story of medieval Nuremberg, *The Mastersingers*, 1868) or the superhuman, with the mythological figures of his mightiest work, *The Ring of the Nibelung*. Wagner delineated character and indicated plot developments in his music by means of special themes or phrases associated with particular people or elements in the story. The way in which these themes are introduced and combined adds greatly to the dramatic effect of the music, as well as serving to bind the whole conception together in an impressive unity. The full-blown concept of the *Leitmotiv*, as it is called, belongs to Wagner, though the operas of Verdi and Puccini, among others, abound in moments where a theme associated with a particular character or situation is brought back later in the story to great effect, as for instance in the last scene of Puccini's *La Bohème* (1896), where the heroine Mimi is dying and the music recalls her first meeting with the young poet Rodolfo.

A scene from Wagner's opera *The Valkyrie*

There has never been any universally accepted 'form' for opera, as there was for the classical symphony: composers have had to invent musical shapes to match the development of the story. Few have approached the fusion of dramatic and musical form achieved by Wagner, though modern operas in general tend to be much more closely knit as musical entities than was once the case. Alban Berg's *Wozzeck* (1925) is one example of a twentieth-century opera whose musical structure is as taut as its dramatic argument, while the works of such earlier operatic masters as Handel, Gluck, Mozart and Rossini consisted for the most part of sequences of fine solos, duets, quartets, choruses and so forth which shared no connection with each other apart from a fairly close key-relationship.

One of the most fundamental problems of opera is that of linking together musical 'set pieces' which express some important emotional or domestic situation. Composers have greatly varied in their treatment of these linking passages. In earlier operas, a kind of singing-speech called 'recitative' was preferred. Sometimes ordinary speech is employed; in more recent times, the tendency has been for the distinction between recitative and set pieces to disappear, as in the operas of Richard Strauss, where the effect is of a continuing stream of beautiful sound.

It could be argued, perhaps, that music plays a less dominant role in the theatrical art of BALLET, though it is difficult to imagine ballet without music of some kind.

Just as music has from the earliest times played an important part in the drama, so it has always been inseparable from the dance; but the kind of formalized, spectacular dancing that we call ballet did not really develop until the late sixteenth and early seventeenth centuries. At the court of King Louis XIV, Jean-Baptiste Lully (1632–1687) organized highly elaborate entertainments in which gavottes, minuets and other

Modern ballet: *Jazz Calendar*

such dances were performed by the courtiers themselves, and ballets also began to be introduced into opera. Dress was elaborate and copious, and the subject matter of ballet was restricted at this time to mythology.

The story-ballet was really established by Jean Georges Noverre (1727–1810), who also managed to free ballet from some of the established conventions; but new conventions were established soon afterwards – the flowing white dress for women (as worn by the great ballerina Taglioni, who was active from 1822 to 1847), the tights, and the practice of dancing on the 'points', the tips of the toes. The famous ballet *Les Sylphides*, arranged to the music of Chopin, is based on these characteristics of the 'romantic' ballet.

The choreographer (dance-designer) of *Les Sylphides* was Michael Fokine, one of the many brilliant talents assembled by the Russian impresario Serge Diaghilev (1872–1929), whose activities made the early years of the twentieth century the Golden Age of ballet, not least because he had a profound understanding of music and gave the ballet score a new importance as a musical entity.

Before the days of Diaghilev, charm was probably the chief characteristic of ballet music; and charming indeed was the ballet music of, for example, Léo Delibes (*Coppélia* 1870, *Sylvia* 1876), though we must add that Tchaikovsky's ballets *The Nutcracker*, *The Sleeping Beauty* and *Swan Lake* are in a high class of their own. But Diaghilev gave ballet music a new dimension when he commissioned such *avant-garde* men as Igor Stravinsky (see page 135) and Maurice Ravel (1875–1937) to compose ballets for him. Stravinsky's *The Rite of Spring*, first staged as a ballet in 1913, has tremendous importance in the development of music, and created a sensation at the time, through what was thought to be the dissonance and savagery of the music. It is a comment on changing taste that sixty years later *The Rite of Spring* is an accepted concert-hall favourite, though it retains its power to thrill. Another great Stravinsky ballet score was *Petrushka* (1911), about a fairground puppet who comes to life, while Ravel's *Daphnis and Chloë* (1912) is another glorious ballet score which now forms a regular part of the orchestral repertoire. Since the days of Diaghilev, many more fine original scores have been created for ballet – Prokofiev's *Romeo and Juliet* and *Cinderella*, *Job* by Ralph Vaughan Williams (1872–1958) and *The Spider's Banquet* by Albert Roussel (1869–1937) come immediately to mind – and many existing scores have been adapted for the ballet.

In this chapter we have surveyed very briefly a selection of important musical forms. In the most extensive sonata or symphony, in the most imposing opera or ballet score, you will find, if you look, evidence of the six germinal musical patterns we mentioned earlier; but those who set out to explore the wide musical world will not confine themselves to the mechanism of music.

6
Enjoying Music

About the middle of September each year, a strange thing happens in South Kensington, London. The Royal Albert Hall is besieged for several days and nights by a youthful army of enthusiasts queuing for admission to the Last Night of the Proms. This extraordinary musical orgy signals the end of two months' music-making in the Promenade Concerts, featuring the world's finest orchestras, soloists and conductors and some of the most *avant-garde* kinds of music as well as the established repertoire.

In a queue outside the hall, the 'Promenaders' – who will stand throughout the concert – sit or sprawl on the pavement, equipped with sleeping bags to ward off the chill winds of the London night, camping stoves to brew up tea or coffee, strange hats and blankets and transistor radios. They talk incessantly, welcoming new arrivals whether they come from up the road or California or New Zealand.

When the doors open, about half an hour before the concert is due to begin, the Promenaders make a mad dash to secure a place 'on the rail', the brass barrier which, in the great central arena of the hall, separates them from the performers. There then begins a pandemonium of whistle-blowing, shouting, singing and stamping. When the members of the orchestra come on, they are soon struggling to free themselves from a wild tangle of streamers; the leader gets enormous acclaim and the conductor a deafening ovation. Then, he raises his baton – and a quite extraordinary thing happens.

There is total silence.

Hardly a cough or a rustle disturbs the course of the opening music. Then once again that vociferous uproar, followed again by silence as the music proceeds. Only in the second half of the programme does the audience itself get a chance to make music, in patriotic songs sung in the name of good humour and good companionship.

Is this 'enjoying music'?

Without any doubt it is enjoyment. And, although some people argue that such orgiastic proceedings have nothing to do with music, there is probably no agent other than music which could bring together such a vast concourse of people (the concert is shared by about a hundred million people around the world through radio and television) and make them forget their differences for a while in the sheer joy of living. There is no better way of enjoying music than in the company of others at a 'live' performance.

No better way – but of course music can nowadays be enjoyed in other

Russian boys enjoying the production of music

ways too, which bring their own special rewards, thanks to the enormous technical advances made during recent years in methods of reproduction. Various systems now exist which go well beyond two-speaker stereo listening, with its illusion of depth and position, to multiple-speaker arrangements which create to a staggering extent a 'you are there' impression. Some are alarmed by these developments, suspecting that the live concert will soon be a thing of the past, though in fact attendances at concerts have grown rather than diminished as a result of the new familiarity with the repertoire brought about by gramophone and radio. And, in any case, the two experiences are complementary.

King Oliver's jazz band in the twenties

Igor Stravinsky considered it bad to listen to music with your eyes closed; better, he thought, to be aware of the actual physical process of music-making, which for him was all part of the enjoyment of music. But many people actually prefer listening to music in the undistracted peace and quiet of their homes.

After music in the concert hall and music in the home, music in the open air provides a third kind of special enjoyment. Here there are the distractions of the surroundings. But how enchanting the total effect can be! – whether of madrigals sung in punts on the river at Cambridge on a summer evening; or of a symphony orchestra performing in the Hollywood Bowl or beside the lake in London's Kenwood at dusk; or (thanks to car radio and cassette machines) of music by Elgar heard while driving through the Malvern Hills where he spent so much of his life.

In fact, the only way *not* to enjoy hearing music is to try to do something contradictory at the same time. There are ways of giving yourself not only mentally but physically to music by doing other things as well as listening; by marching to music, for instance, performing physical exercises to it, skating to it, or dancing to it. In such ways we almost become part of the music through movement.

And this gives us the clue to the best way of all to enjoy music – by taking part in it as a performer or 'active listener'. If you learn to play an instrument or to sing, then you will of course learn a great deal in the process about musical enjoyment. If not, well, you can clap or stamp in rhythm like the audience at the Last Night of the Proms, and join in the choruses. And whatever the extent of your participation in music-making, you can greatly enrich the experience with a little reading and careful listening.

The programme notes in concert programmes often provide a start in musical appreciation, though if you know well in advance that you are going to a concert, it's obviously a good idea to do a bit of reading beforehand. Nowadays a good many handy encyclopedias and dictionaries of

The Rolling Stones

music are produced in paperback. You are hardly likely to possess the huge Grove's *Dictionary of Music and Musicians* unless you are a professional or a dedicated amateur, but it's always well worth consulting at a public library, which nowadays may also have a record library to lend you records of the works you are about to hear. The record will probably have a 'sleeve note'; and you will have the advantage, through listening to the record, of familiarizing yourself with the material. One of the great pleasures of music is the pleasure of recognition, and one of the tests of a fine piece of music is how often you want to hear it again: in the case of many favourite works, almost inexhaustibly. Study of a work from a gramophone record is, of course, greatly aided if you can read a printed copy of the composer's 'score'. In the case of many standard works, such scores are available in pocket size and are not very expensive.

If you happen to be going to the opera rather than a concert, it is essential to have as detailed a knowledge of the story as possible, particularly if the opera is being sung in a foreign language. Many operatic records have the libretto with a line-by-line translation printed on a leaflet inserted into the record sleeve, and this is invaluable when listening to a recorded opera for the first time. If a recording with libretto is not available, then you can find the plots of many operas admirably outlined in a number of books: one of the most famous is Kobbé's *Complete Opera Book*.

It may at first thought seem a passive occupation to attend a concert or an opera, but even though not all audiences are quite so extrovert in their responses as London's Promenaders, the mental and emotional participation of the audience is of the utmost importance if the performance is to be a success. Music is a form of communication, and communication is a two-way business; from the quality of attention in the theatre or hall, a performer draws either inspiration or discouragement. So even though you think of yourself as 'just a listener' to music, your share in the act of musical re-creation is of vital importance.

From a thirteenth-century psalter: King David as a harpist, with players of a viol, a trumpet, a percussion instrument and bagpipes

7
How Music Grew
From the Middle Ages to the Classical Period

The history of music is, like the history of man, a story of rebels and reactionaries. Over and over again we read of the struggle of those who advocated the 'new music' against those who held to the old forms. The struggle was in fact continuous over the centuries, but we are most strongly aware of it at certain periods – for example, during what we call the Renaissance, the awakening from the Church-dominated Middle Ages, and again during the period towards the end of the eighteenth century which roughly coincides with the French Revolution and all it implied.

Of course, all historical labels are suspect, and although in these two chapters we shall divide and label musical history to some extent, we do so to provide a few landmarks in a vast area of knowledge, in the hope that the reader will be tempted to question and explore further.

The Middle Ages
Before the growth of a distinctively American culture, the story of Western music is essentially the story of European music, and like most aspects of European civilization, it owed a great deal to ideas inherited from the Ancient World – the civilizations of Greece and Rome. It might be said that the germinal spirit of Western music was the philosopher Pythagoras, for he and his followers established all the musical intervals known to us, on mathematical principles related, they believed, to the structure of the Universe itself. They bequeathed to Europe the concept of music as a reflection of the Divine Order of things – an idea that recurred frequently in Western philosophy – and presented the Christian Church with the system of modes which were the technical basis of music in classical Greece.

Music played a central part in ancient Greek civilization at its height (the sixth and fifth centuries B.C.). The philosopher Plato used the word 'music' to embrace the whole field of mental and spiritual culture – singing, poetry, instrumental performances, dancing and oratory: activities which featured in religious festivals, and were brought together in the growth of classical Greek drama. In great open amphitheatres, some of whose ruins remain, the plays were performed by groups of artists who could sing, act and dance, the dances taking place in the central arena in front of the raised stage called, after the Greek word for dance, the 'orchestra'. That word, together with the myths that were the basis of Greek drama, re-emerged in the history of European music somewhere around the year 1600 when opera was born, and looked for its subject matter to the ancients: this was fully in keeping with the spirit of the Renaissance, which in so many ways was a rediscovery of the spirit of pre-Christian antiquity.

Just before the beginning of the Christian era, the Greek city states fell to the advancing Roman Empire, which adopted the manner of Greek drama and music without its feeling. As time went on, the status of music declined from a semi-religious activity to mere amusement, and loud indeed were the condemnations of it by the early fathers of the Church. Anything which recalled the decadence of the theatre was banned, and, in keeping with St Augustine's fear of taking more pleasure in singing than in what was actually sung, the early Church developed a spare pure style for its psalms and hymns.

This style probably owed less to the Greek tradition than to the Jewish, for the first Christians were of course Jews, and they frequently adopted the methods of chanting psalms and intoning the scriptures which were used in the Hebrew temples. Such were the beginnings of the great body of early Christian Church music known as PLAINSONG, which, in its greatest period (from the fifth to the eighth centuries A.D.) became a matchless vehicle for conveying religious truth. This art developed in the monasteries, which were the chief centres of culture in the period following the collapse of the Roman Empire in the West around A.D. 400: its object was to convey the meaning of the words with the utmost clarity and conviction, and it was therefore restricted to a single line of melody, intoned by a soloist with a choral refrain, or by two sections of a choir singing alternately. There was no accompaniment, and in the purest form of plainsong no kind of decoration. We cannot be quite sure what plainsong sounded like in those early days, owing to the inadequacy of musical notation at that time, but the effect of plainsong as performed today is attractively austere, haunting and other-worldly.

In time composers began to emerge from the anonymity of the cloister, and the name of the Franco-Flemish monk Hucbald (c. A.D. 840–930) has come down to us as one of the earliest Europeans to write fine music. The artistic activities of the ninth and tenth centuries are sometimes referred to as the Carolingian Renaissance, a label derived from the descendants of the Emperor Charles the Great (Charlemagne), who ruled over a great area of Europe around the year A.D. 800. It was a time above all of beautifully produced manuscript books – scriptural and historical texts, together with Latin classics and poetry; and the development by Guido of Arezzo of the staff system of notation may be regarded as part of this great upsurge of communication through the art of writing.

It was at this time that the practice grew up of repeating certain phrases of melody at the interval of a fourth or a fifth above the original pitch, and from there the way was open for the development of 'singing in harmony' or POLYPHONY, which means a musical texture that is 'many-sounded' or 'many-voiced'. At first the voices moved in parallel, at a set interval apart, but soon they began to move more freely, above long-held notes

Tudor musicians performing in church

supplied by various musical instruments, most notably the organ.

This kind of music, which came to be known as ORGANUM from the Latin name for an instrument of any kind, and also for the organ itself, was prevalent in the Europe of the eleventh and twelfth centuries. Styles varied, which is not surprising in an age when travel was difficult and the great ecclesiastical centres of Europe were widely separated. The most remarkable musical centre was unquestionably Paris. At Notre Dame, in the latter part of the twelfth century, Léonin and his successor Pérotin introduced new kinds of rhythmic and melodic flexibility into Church music which led on to the thirteenth-century MOTET (the name derived from the French *mot*, meaning 'word'), a form lending itself to florid variations over a sustained lower part, the 'tenor'.

It was no new thing to introduce secular melodies into Church music – St Ambrose, in the fourth century, is supposed to have assured the popularity of his hymns by basing them on Italian folk melodies; but during the thirteenth century the practice grew apace. Outside the Church, the chief exponents of music were the minstrels or JONGLEURS, a French word related to the Latin *joculator*, meaning an entertainer. And entertainers they were. Travelling the continent in pairs or groups, they could offer their audiences a variety of diversions not only as acrobats, jugglers, jesters, story-tellers and actors, but also as singers and instrumental

performers. Their musical repertoire consisted of popular dances and
songs, which often enough reversed the borrowing process and made use
of themes from the Church repertory. Part songs too began to be written
in the twelfth and thirteenth centuries, though the tradition of part singing in folk song was already firmly established in Scotland, Ireland,
Wales, and northern England, where children were said to be able to sing
in parts from infancy, and where inborn musical talent is specially marked
to this day.

Towards the end of the eleventh century, in southern France, and over
the next two hundred years, the art of the minstrel was given an
aristocratic refinement by the TROUBADOURS, some of them knightly
figures like Bernard de Ventadorn, who made poetry and music part of
chivalry, employing them more often than not to express the delights and
despairs of love. Similar, in the north, were the TROUVÈRES, of whom
Adam de la Halle is one of the best known, together with Blondel de Nesle,
who is supposed to have rescued Richard I from imprisonment after a
Crusade. The art of courtly song was practised in Germany by the
aristocratic MINNESINGERS, later to become the professional mastersingers who organized themselves into carefully regulated guilds, and
were celebrated in the great opera by Wagner which is named after
them. Fortunately, there has been a great revival of interest in early
music in recent years and several instrumental and vocal groups perform
it.

The fourteenth century was, in more ways than one, a period of
transition. The knightly ideals of the Middle Ages, identified as they
were with the concept of service to a lady, a feudal lord, or to God, began
to crumble, as powerful kings such as Philip IV of France and Edward III
of England battled for supremacy; even the Pope became the plaything
of the big battalions. Music was part of political one-up-man-ship, and
the great princes vied with each other for the services of leading musicians.
Singing and dancing would often follow evening meals, with musicians
up in the minstrels' gallery performing on such instruments as the shawm
or bagpipe, the bombard (a large oboe) and the slide trumpet. The viol
and the portable or 'portative' organ were popular too, as were the
cornet, recorder and flute. By the end of the fourteenth century, vocal
music had become highly ornate – in itself a sign of the ostentation
thought desirable by potentates; and the two leading composers of the
time, Philippe de Vitry and Guillaume de Machaut, were extravagantly
praised as respectively the 'flower and jewel of musicians' and the
'earthly god of harmony'.

The rhythm of plainsong was no doubt a fluid affair, though governed
by well-defined tradition. Vitry now invented much more definite ways
of indicating rhythm, introducing the kind of time signatures – $\frac{9}{8}, \frac{6}{8}, \frac{3}{4}, \frac{2}{4}$,
and the rest – which we recognize today. With mathematical precision,
he divided and subdivided note-values, to give us our semi-breves and
minims, and laid down new rules of rhythmic emphasis. On this basis

Singers of the fifteenth century

Guillaume de Machaut and others produced many attractive works of great brilliance and ingenuity, in which perhaps perfection of form seems more important than profundity of meaning.

The Renaissance

The period of the Renaissance in musical terms is usually taken to extend between 1400 and 1600. By a very gradual process, and by methods which varied in different parts of Europe, music gradually came, over that period of two hundred years, to assume shapes which are recognizably modern. They relate to a world we can understand much more easily than the medieval one, for the Renaissance spirit questioned the all-pervading authority of the Church, reasserting man's capacity to think for himself. Geographical discovery, scientific experiment, daring

architecture, power politics; poetry, painting and sculpture which show
a reawakened interest in the human form; a rebirth of interest in the pre-
Christian civilizations of Greece and Rome – all these are the marks of
what we call the Renaissance, together with musical developments which
shifted the emphasis to some extent from the Church to court and stately
home, and from France to Italy and England, and brought a new awareness of instrumental music and a sense of participation, caused by the
spread of printed music and more accessible kinds of musical structure.

Hitherto the plainsong chant, with decorative additions, had been the
basis of Church music: now there grew up for the first time part singing
as we know it, with a democratic equality between the various 'voices'.
It was around 1460 that the first 'part books' came into use in choirs.

Such composers as the English John Dunstable and the Flemish
Guillaume Dufay and Josquin des Prés enjoyed a status far above that of
the ordinary minstrels who were employed in large numbers at court.
Minstrels were required to provide suitably rousing music when their
masters were engaged on martial enterprises, and to accompany the
'basse-danse', the 'branle' and the 'pavane', together with other dances
which successively became the rage. Minstrelsy was an important craft,
and in 1469 a guild was set up in England to regulate its affairs. Most
minstrels were able to turn their hands to a number of instruments, but
towards the end of the century, there grew up a new kind of performer,
the virtuoso of the organ – and, later, other keyboard instruments – who
could expect a distinguished welcome wherever he went.

The Italian writer Castiglione considered music an essential accom-
plishment of the courtier, and the English composer Thomas Morley
believed that, if a man could not sing a madrigal part at sight, it was a
sign of a poor education. The madrigal, as a highly developed part song
for unaccompanied voices, came to the fore in Italy in the early part of the
century, and indeed it was in Italy that many of the most interesting
developments of the period took place. The splendour of the papal
establishment in Rome was rivalled by Florence under the Medicis and
the spectacular ceremonial of Venice, and each had its musicians to add
to the pomp. People began to attend concerts just for the sake of listening
to music, which was something quite new; professional musicians
flourished, and there was a growing demand for pieces which could either
be sung, or performed by a group of instruments. Madrigal writers were
specially attentive to the meaning of words, aiming to make their music
expressive of every turn of emotion; and later in the century in Italy the
madrigal was sometimes used to paint a descriptive picture, such as 'The
Chattering of the Women at the Laundry' (1567). This development led
in Venice to the beginnings of opera.

The greatest Italian composer of the time, Giovanni Palestrina
(1525–1594), wrote very few madrigals, but as many as one hundred and
five masses, notable for their serenity of mood and beautiful melodic
shape; hardly less distinguished was his friend, the Spaniard Tomás de

The Last Night of the Proms.
OVERLEAF Unconventional music-making in seventeenth-century Holland

Victoria (1549–1611), who spent much of his life in Rome. Other great Church composers of the period were the Englishmen Thomas Tallis (1505–1585) and William Byrd (1543–1623). Byrd, who remained a Roman Catholic, was nevertheless one of the first great composers of the Anglican Church, which in the mid-sixteenth century established its independence from Rome and required a new repertoire of Church music as a result. The anthems of Byrd, and his younger contemporaries Weelkes and Orlando Gibbons, are often exquisitely beautiful. So too is the music of the greatest Flemish master of the period, Lassus, or Orlando di Lasso, who lived from 1532 to 1594.

The second half of the sixteenth century brought a marvellous flowering of music in England which matches in splendour the poetry of Shakespeare, Marlowe, Spenser and Sidney. Apart from the magnificent Church music of Byrd and others, the English madrigal in the hands of such composers as Morley, Wilbye and Weelkes became a vehicle for some of the most expressive music ever written; the songs of John Dowland (1563–1626) and others have lost none of their eloquence. A major innovation was the appearance of books of dances and fantasies specifically written or arranged for certain instruments, among which the lute was extremely popular, as were the organ, the virginals (an early harpsichord), viols and recorders.

The Baroque Period

The century and a half of artistic development between approximately 1600 and 1750 is often described by the adjective Baroque, which literally means 'bizarre'. Derived from the Spanish word *barrueco*, 'an irregularly-shaped pearl', it was first applied to the architecture of the period, with its proliferation of ornament, and then extended to its elaborate paintings and music.

Drama is one of the most important strands in the development of Baroque music. The period saw the growth of opera together with its religious equivalent, ORATORIO, and a great development of instrumental music which led on to those essentially dramatic musical forms, the classical symphony and sonata.

When this period began, most musical activity outside the Church was confined to the homes of the very rich, but by the 1650s public operatic performances were being given. In 1672 the first public concerts were heard in London, to be followed by similar ventures in Germany and France.

Opera – the concept of setting a dramatic story to music – had a double origin. Since the very early Middle Ages, music had played a great part in the 'miracle' or 'mystery' plays which were performed in church or street; on the other hand, in the many revivals of classical plays during the Renaissance, musical interludes became an increasingly popular feature. From there it was no great step, perhaps, to the first full-scale opera, Peri's *La Dafne* ('Daphne'), which was first performed in Florence

Festive dancing in England and China

in 1597. This was a mythological story of nymphs and satyrs, as were many early operas. Cavalieri's *Representation of Soul and Body* of 1602, on the other hand, pointed the way to the religious themes of oratorio. The first great opera composer was Claudio Monteverdi (1567–1643), and his *Orpheus* (1607) employed the 'colour' of orchestral instruments to portray character – an essential feature of operatic composition – and established the distinction between RECITATIVE (a kind of musical recitation which allows the performer to act expressively and thus advance the plot) and the ARIA, which is a set piece, often expressing an emotional state.

In Rome, drama-with-music advanced towards oratorio, while in Venice the first Opera House opened in 1637. There, Monteverdi's *The Coronation of Poppea* introduced to the operatic scene that strange operatic monster the 'castrato', or male adult soprano, a type of singer who achieved almost 'pop star' status and success over the next century. Even more significantly, Monteverdi introduced in one of his dramatic cantatas the distribution of stringed instruments – first and second violins, violas, cellos and double basses – which was to form the basis of the modern orchestra. As to style of presentation, some Venetian operas were sparing of resources; others were vastly elaborate, like Marcantonio Cesti's *Il Pomo d'Oro* ('The Golden Apple') composed in 1667, which called for sixty-seven scenes and no fewer than twenty-four stage settings.

If Venice pioneered opera in the first part of the seventeenth century. Naples occupied the centre of the stage in the second half. Neapolitan OPERA SERIA, 'serious opera', had extremely artificial plots, though at least one major composer made them live: Alessandro Scarlatti (1660–1725). But a second kind of opera also flourished in Naples in the late seventeenth and early eighteenth centuries: OPERA BUFFA, a form of entertainment more concerned with real-life characters, usually strong in comedy. This kind of opera was to be the pattern of some of Mozart's finest works.

Italian influence was supreme in European music at this time. For a while France stood out against the fashion, but Jean Baptiste Lully (1632–1687), who was Italian born, changed that. His work, however, took on a distinctively French character; a much less elaborate vocal line, greater dramatic intensity. These qualities were also exhibited by Lully's greatest successor, Jean Philippe Rameau (1683–1764). In the mid-eighteenth century an artistic war broke out between the 'Ramists' and the admirers of Neapolitan opera buffa, which had just invaded the French capital; serious Rameau-type opera triumphed and, in such works as *Orpheus and Eurydice* and *Alcestis* by Christoph Willibald von Gluck (1714–1787), it achieved heroic dignity and beauty.

Perhaps the supreme non-Italian exponent of Italian opera was George Frederic Handel (see page 112), who had enormous success in London in the early eighteenth century with his many works in opera seria style, influenced no doubt by a three-year visit to Italy. The English native

Sixteenth-century Holland: playing the harpsichord

tradition of musical drama had developed meanwhile along rather different lines, growing out of the elaborate masques of such men as Ben Jonson and Inigo Jones under King James I and Charles I into the many fine stage works of Henry Purcell (see page 107), only one of which, *Dido and Aeneas* (*c.* 1689), was strictly speaking an opera; the remainder were adaptations of plays with a substantial element of music and dance – in some ways not unlike twentieth-century stage musicals. The English equivalent of opera buffa appeared in 1728 with John Gay's *The Beggar's Opera*. A tale of low-life villains, it was the first of the 'ballad' operas, and its witty blend of words and music established a kind of musical entertainment that has ever since been popular in Britain.

The talents of both Purcell and Handel as dramatic composers found another outlet in Church music, building on the traditions of anthem composition established by William Byrd and others.

In Handel's case, the experience he had gained in the opera house undoubtedly sharpened the dramatic effect of his great oratorios, especially the supreme *Messiah* of 1741. In Germany, the Lutheran Church developed the CHORALE, a dignified hymn-tune designed for the congregation to sing; and this provided a wonderful basis for more elaborate Church compositions. Heinrich Schütz (1585–1672) wrote the first German opera as well as the earliest German oratorios, whose dramatic alternation of soloists, ensembles, and great choruses anticipated Johann Sebastian Bach (see page 108).

Bach wrote hundreds of CANTATAS (mini-oratorios designed for particular days of the Church year), as well as his mighty full-scale oratorios, such as the *St John Passion* and *St Matthew Passion* and the *Mass in B Minor*. Bach's music is often highly dramatic. His numerous trills and other ornaments are always subordinate to the main argument; he could handle large vocal and instrumental forces with consummate skill. Together with his exact contemporary Handel, he shows us Baroque musical architecture at its imposing best.

That Bach was also a superb keyboard performer, notably on the organ and harpsichord, is also a significant fact in the story of Baroque composition, which is marked by a rapid development of all kinds of instrumental music. Other great harpsichord composer-performers of the period were the French François Couperin (1668–1733), who produced a great variety of descriptive pieces grouped in *ordres* or SUITES, and the Italian Domenico Scarlatti (1685–1757), whose hundreds of brilliant harpsichord sonatas helped to point the way to the sonata form of the later eighteenth century.

Meanwhile the word 'sonata', in the seventeenth century, whether qualified as 'da camera' or 'da chiesa', could mean many different things, often enough a sequence of dance movements. Sometimes sonatas were written for a single instrument; very frequently they were 'trio sonatas', which typically employed two violins and a harpsichord CONTINUO or linking accompaniment, though they could be performed on other instruments, or by a larger group of performers. The boundary between chamber music and orchestral music was virtually undefined: in England in the early seventeenth century the FANTASIA for strings was a pioneering form, but in orchestral as in vocal music the most significant innovations of the period came from Italy.

It was there that the sinfonia of the Opera House (where, as we have seen, the name was applied to what we would now call an overture or INTERMEZZO) was first used to describe an independent instrumental composition, and there that the CONCERTO GROSSO was developed in the hands of such composers as Corelli, Stradella, Torelli, Albinoni, and most notably of all Antonio Vivaldi (*c.* 1678–1741). They used small groups of instruments set against the full orchestra, or followed the new fashion established in the first decade of the eighteenth century of writing for a single solo instrument and orchestra.

The Classical Period

People often use the phrase 'classical music' to describe the whole field of serious music that is not 'light', 'jazz', 'pop' or 'folk', musical territories which in themselves are fairly ill-defined. But classical music, using the term more strictly, really belongs to a quite limited period of time, the last years of the eighteenth century and the very beginning of the nineteenth. It is the kind of music produced supremely by Haydn (see page 114), Mozart (page 116) and Beethoven (page 117), though Beethoven occupies a pivotal position, leaning in much of his work towards the 'romantic' movement in music which dominated the nineteenth century and is still, some would say, an active force in composition.

'Classical' is a word used to describe most artistic forms at a certain stage in their development, and refers back to the art of classical Greece. The Parthenon, like the plays of Aeschylus and Euripides, exhibits the perfectly balanced shape which is one of the most marked features of 'classical' art at all periods. But a balanced shape does not imply lack of passion. Quite the contrary. Ancient Greek plays such as the *Agamemnon* and *Oedipus Rex* are concerned with colossal passions, but they are presented with restraint. This, if anything, enhances the effect. There is a burning tension in classical drama which results from the exercise of strong control over powerful material. And this tension is to be found, too, in 'classical' music.

In France, opera reached a point of classical splendour with Gluck's great works *Orpheus* (1762), *Alcestis* (1767), *Iphigenia in Aulis* (1774) and *Iphigenia in Tauris* (1779), which all treated Greek tragic themes with a Greek economy of style. This was opera seria given real substance and power; but with Gluck it remained a quite distinct category. It was left to Mozart to bring together the nobility of opera seria and the humanity of opera buffa. Mozart's operas *The Marriage of Figaro* (1786), *The Magic Flute* (1791), *Don Giovanni* (1787) and *Così Fan Tutte* (1790) are among the greatest works of art in any medium: as great in their range of human sympathy as in their perfection of form.

That Mozart should choose *The Marriage of Figaro* as one of his subjects is highly significant, for the play (by the French writer Beaumarchais) on which it is based tells the story of a disrespectful valet who thinks himself every bit as good as his 'betters'; the same character appears in that other notable Beaumarchais play, *The Barber of Seville*, on which Rossini founded one of his operas. These plays caused a storm of outrage from the King and the aristocracy in the Paris of the 1780s and were ingredients of the intellectual atmosphere which led to the French Revolution of 1789. Clearly Mozart was open to the liberalizing influences of his time.

Meanwhile the sinfonia of the Opera House had broken out into the concert room, and in 1740 the Austrian composer Georg Matthias Monn wrote the first known symphony in four movements. Early symphonies were lightweight affairs in general, and there was no firmly established form for them, any more than there was for the SERENADE or the DIVERTIMENTO – sequences of contrasting pieces designed to provide pleasant entertainment at supper parties and so forth. Meanwhile, in Madrid, no doubt to amuse and instruct his royal patrons, Domenico Scarlatti was producing the bulk of his six hundred keyboard sonatas, short, brilliant pieces which pioneered the use of two contrasting themes in sonata-form first movements.

What may be called the first 'symphony orchestra' was at work in Mannheim, North Germany, from about 1740 under the patronage of the Elector, the Duke Carl Theodor. The orchestra, which was highly influential, gave concerts in public, and it became famous throughout the musical world for the brilliance and flexibility of its playing. At about the same time, at the court of Frederick the Great of Prussia, Carl Philipp Emanuel Bach (1714–1788), second son of Johann Sebastian Bach, was introducing a quite new element of personal expression into the French musical fashions of the Court. C. P. E. Bach proclaimed that ornament – the dominating feature of Rococo ('Ornate') art in all its forms – must play its part in the musical structure as a whole. There are signs of a new emotional turbulence in his work which point forward to Beethoven, but this, too, is finely controlled in sonata movements which were among the first to realize the dramatic potential of the form.

These sonatas were a great source of inspiration to Haydn, who said he owed everything he knew to C. P. E. Bach. But in his sonatas and symphonies, Haydn developed sonata-form into something altogether grander and more significant, though never losing the common touch. Fresh ideas and variety of treatment mark all Haydn's best work, and in the twelve 'London' symphonies we find the classical symphony at its zenith. Of Mozart's symphonies, the last three, written in six weeks in the summer of 1788, show him at his supreme best, exhibiting a sharp intensity of feeling which Haydn perhaps does not share, though the form of the Mozartian symphony is by comparison conventional. With his operatic genius, Mozart was more of an innovator in the field of the concerto (in particular the piano concerto), which after all can be thought of as the operatic aria in concert form. As Haydn had done with the symphony, Mozart developed the concerto from a decorative display into a dramatic dialogue between soloist and orchestra. Both men were masters of chamber-music forms, notably the STRING QUARTET; but it was Haydn who took the lead in transforming what had been the vehicle for a street serenade into perhaps the most profound and intimate form of musical expression which has yet been invented.

In his quartets, as in his symphonies and sonatas, Beethoven started where Haydn left off. With Beethoven, music ceases altogether to salute

A musical gathering at the time of Mozart

the autocrat – here is the man of the French Revolution asserting his right to be heard, if necessary at the top of his voice. Classical restraint begins to be undermined by personal expression and affirmation: we feel it in Beethoven's single great opera *Fidelio*, deeply concerned as it is with the rights of Man as against the System, in his immense Masses in C and D major as well as in the sonata-form works. And towards the end, with Beethoven, especially in the late piano sonatas and string quartets, we hear a quite different and, in a way, an even more personal voice, a quiet mystical voice which, out of the still centre of the *Sturm und Drang* ('storm and stress'), speaks of a serenity and peace which passes human understanding. Beethoven was recognized as a titanic figure even by his contemporaries and successors. He was to become, in fact, one of the great romantic heroes of the romantic movement.

8

How Music Grew
From the Romantic Age to the Present Day

The term 'romantic' is no less difficult to define than 'classical', and in attempting to do so we must say at once that there is no hard-and-fast division between these two areas of music, any more than there is between any of the other categories we have been considering. But the spirit of music-making does change throughout the years, and the nineteenth century is associated with the expression of personal feeling in music to a greater extent than previous ages. The romantics invented new shapes for their music which answered to their own inner need – shapes which ballooned into the immense operas of Richard Wagner (see page 129), and the huge symphonic structures of Anton Bruckner (1824–1896) and Gustav Mahler (see page 139); but subjective thoughts and feelings were also the guiding force in more intimate forms of music, such as piano pieces.

If there is any one instrument which is associated more than any other with romantic music, it is the pianoforte. Upright pianos first appeared in Britain and the United States at the very beginning of the nineteenth century, and as the century went on they became an indispensable part of almost every household – a highly significant fact in the musical life of the period.

Certainly the piano was significant to Franz Schubert (see page 120). Although he died only a year after Beethoven, he seems to belong essentially among the romantics. Schubert wrote a great many beautiful works on a large scale, but it is perhaps for his exquisitely expressive songs (he wrote no fewer than six hundred and three) that he is historically most important. He is the first great figure in the history of the German *Lied* ('art song'), which brought a new dramatic sensibility to the merging of poetry and music. The piano part is quite indispensable in songs such as Schubert's: like the orchestra in opera, it often supplies the 'colour' of the composition; and if the atmosphere of these marvellous miniatures is to be conveyed to an audience, the pianist must be every bit as fine an artist as the singer, a fact that has led a number of good pianists to devote their careers entirely to accompanying.

Robert Schumann (see page 123) concentrated entirely on the piano as a young man, expressing in attractive works like *Papillons* ('Butterflies') and *Carnaval* his own highly individual imagination; and the piano part was of great importance in the many beautiful songs he wrote after his marriage to the pianist Clara Wieck. Johannes Brahms (see page 124), befriended by the Schumanns as a young man, was also a magnificent pianist who produced two of the mightiest of all piano concertos, much

Nicolò Paganini

chamber music involving the piano and a great many deeply expressive songs and piano solos.

One of the most influential figures in nineteenth-century music was Franz Liszt (1811–1886), its most astonishing virtuoso of the pianoforte, though it should perhaps be mentioned that the ultimate in romantic virtuosity, and a source of inspiration to Liszt and many others, was the brilliant violinist Nicolò Paganini (1782–1840). After giving a concert in Vienna at the age of eleven, Liszt received the accolade of a kiss from Beethoven, and very soon went on to conquer the salons of Europe with his Hungarian good looks and dazzling technique. He was lionized especially in Paris, as was that other emigré from eastern Europe, the Polish-born Frédéric Chopin. Through his waltzes, nocturnes, studies and scherzos, Chopin confided a world of personal feeling to the piano-forte, and indeed scarcely composed at all for any other instrument.

Although a musician's potential sources of income were no longer con-fined entirely to the great houses, as they had been in the eighteenth century, artists like Chopin and Liszt depended primarily on aristocratic patronage, and their bravura style of playing owed a great deal to the influence of the GRAND OPERA which was so fashionable in Paris and elsewhere in the first half of the nineteenth century. Showy transcriptions of popular operatic numbers formed an important part of the virtuoso's repertoire – a tribute to the success of such composers as Vincenzo Bellini (1801–1835), Gioacchino Rossini (1792–1868), Gasparo Spontini (1774–1851), Luigi Cherubini (1760–1842) and Giacomo Meyerbeer (1791–1864), all born outside France but attracted to Paris for a major part of their lives.

It was as a composer of opera buffa that Rossini excelled – one has only to think of such comic masterpieces as *The Barber of Seville*, *Cinderella*, and *Count Ory*. But soon after he came to Paris in 1828 he conformed to the taste of the French capital by producing his one and only grand opera, *William Tell*. Enormously successful in his day was Meyerbeer, who gratified the French taste for grandiose spectacle with such works as *Robert the Devil* (1831), *The Huguenots* (1836) and *The Prophet* (1849).

The greatest operatic composer at work in the Paris of the early nineteenth century was not recognized as such in his own time: he was the Frenchman Hector Berlioz (1803-1869). In his brilliant and voluminous memoirs, Berlioz tells us how his highly developed romantic imagination reacted when he first read Virgil's *Aeneid*. The experience almost shattered him, and it resulted after many years of struggle in the great opera *The Trojans*, which was only performed in part during the composer's lifetime; it is only through recent performances that it is now recognized for the masterpiece it is. Berlioz wrote other compositions for the stage, and many of his non-theatrical works are operatic in quality, among them the sensational *Requiem Mass* (which at one point requires four brass bands to thunder out over chorus and orchestra), the 'Fantastic' and 'Romeo and Juliet' symphonies, and the beautiful and deeply moving oratorio *The Childhood of Christ*.

Only one nineteenth-century operatic composer outdid Berlioz in the immensity of his ideas: Richard Wagner (see page 129). Though his achievement is of worldwide importance, Wagner represents, among other things, the nationalistic strand in nineteenth-century music which finds expression in a number of composers and countries. Although *The Flying Dutchman*, *Tannhäuser* and *Lohengrin* had already been staged with success, it was not until after 1848, when Wagner was forced into exile through his 'liberal sympathies' with the revolutionary activities of that year, that he began – with the invaluable support of Franz Liszt, then conductor at Weimar – to produce the works which would most fully express his beliefs about the musical theatre: the four operas which make up *The Ring of the Nibelung* – *The Rhinegold*, *The Valkyrie*, *Siegfried* and *The Twilight of the Gods*, all performed as one cycle for the first time in 1876 – together with *Tristan and Isolde* (1859), *The Mastersingers* (1867) and *Parsifal* (1882). Wagner consciously designed these great works as successors to the symphony of Beethoven; and there are those who regard

Tristan and Isolde as Wagner's greatest symphony. Its harmony was thought revolutionary at the time, and the beginnings of modern music are often traced back to the opening notes of the *Tristan* Prelude.

Giuseppe Verdi (see page 131), the greatest Italian operatic master of the nineteenth century, and one of the most splendid of all composers, had no wish to parallel Wagner's ambition to make music-drama the 'communal expression of the German race', but he was a passionate Italian patriot, much caught up in the Risorgimento, the 'revival' which led to the liberation of Italy from foreign domination and the unification of the country. Gaetano Donizetti (1797–1848), among others, had immense success in the earlier part of the century with works such as *Lucia di Lammermoor* (based on a novel by Walter Scott) and *The Elixir of Love*, but when Verdi's *Nabucco* ('Nebuchadnezzar') reached Milan in 1842, the public at once rose to Verdi's genius, partly because they identified the plight of Italy under the Austrians with that of the Jews exiled in Babylon. Some other Verdi operas had thinly disguised patriotic themes; most of them were highly melodramatic; but whatever the story, Verdi's gifts for melody and characterization brought it to life, as the years went by, with increasing subtlety. Middle-period Verdi operas such as *La Traviata* and *Il Trovatore*, both staged in 1853, *Simon Boccanegra* (1857), *Don Carlos* (1867) and *Aida* (1871) have lost none of their power to thrill an audience; and, in old age, Verdi went on to produce two great masterpieces, *Othello* (1887) and *Falstaff* (1893), music-dramas almost more exciting than Wagner's because closer to ordinary life.

Very much more earthbound than either Verdi or Wagner was Jacques Offenbach (1819–1880), who started a craze for OPÉRA COMIQUE with such irreverent works as *Orpheus in the Underworld*, first produced in Paris in 1858. The craze spread to Vienna, where Franz von Suppé (1819–1895) had great success with many of his one hundred and fifty works, and the second Johann Strauss (1825–1899) scored a hit with *Die Fledermaus*, though he was in general much more successful in the ballroom than in the theatre. In London, the LIGHT OPERAS of Gilbert and Sullivan were the rage in the 1870s and 1880s. But opéra comique does not necessarily mean 'comic opera' to the French, for both *Faust* (1859) by Charles Gounod and *Carmen* (1875) by Georges Bizet, two of the most famous and popular of all operas, come within the same category, as do the attractive works of Jules Massenet (1842–1912) and Ambroise Thomas (1811–1896).

Elsewhere, the operatic stage became the main platform for composers who, like Wagner, wished to give expression to national feelings in their music, notably perhaps in Russia and Bohemia.

Mikhail Glinka (1804–1857) was the first major Russian composer to turn to native sources of inspiration, instead of following the European fashion (mainly French and Italian) as his predecessors had done, and his two operas *A Life for the Tsar* (1836) and *Ruslan and Ludmilla* (1842) are landmarks in the Russian nationalist movement. The supreme achievement of Modeste Moussorgsky (1839–1881) is his *Boris Godounov*; Alexander Borodin (1833–1887) achieved the heroic grandeur of *Prince Igor*; and many people consider the greatest achievement of Peter Ilyich Tchaikovsky (see page 133) was his opera *Eugène Onegin* (1879).

Like the Italians, the people of Bohemia, which together with Moravia and Slovakia is now part of Czechoslovakia, felt oppressed by Austrian rule, and in Bedřich Smetana (1824–1884) they found a musical champion. In operas like *Dalibor* and *Libussa* he gave Wagnerian treatment to nationalistic themes, though it is the comic opera *The Bartered Bride* (1866), bursting with country vitality and colour, by which he is best remembered, together with the patriotic cycle of symphonic poems *Má Vlast* ('My Country'). Antonin Dvořák (see page 126) also added to the Czech operatic repertoire, but he was a cosmopolitan figure, and Smetana's true successor was Leoš Janáček (1854–1928), a composer whose great stature is only now being adequately recognized with international revivals of operas like *Katya Kabanova* and *Jenufa*, and performances of the stark and fascinating *Glagolitic Mass*.

In other countries, too, national awareness found expression in music, though not always in opera. Edvard Grieg (1843–1907) was the first major composer to project a Scandinavian identity, building as he did on the rhythm and melodies of Norwegian folk music; while in Finland, Jean Sibelius, who was born in 1865 but lived through more than half of the twentieth century until his death in 1957, became the embodiment of Finnish musical identity in the struggle against Russian domination: his *Finlandia* (1899) caused a patriotic riot and was banned. Sibelius wrote a number of symphonic poems on national subjects as well as seven major symphonies, which entitle him, in the view of some authorities, to be called the greatest symphonist since Beethoven.

Which brings us back to an important path in the nineteenth-century musical landscape we have not yet pursued.

Like Beethoven himself, Franz Schubert, who died in 1828, the year after Beethoven, also produced nine symphonies, of which No. 8 (the 'Unfinished') and No. 9 (the 'Great C major') are particularly appealing and profound; in many ways his most direct successor was Anton Bruckner (1824–1896), whose eight completed symphonies, some of them immensely long, are melodious in the Schubert fashion. The symphonies of Felix Mendelssohn (see page 121), brilliant and adored by all, not least the British Royal Family, have a more classical tautness of form, as does his exquisite incidental music for *A Midsummer Night's Dream*, written when he was only seventeen, and fine overtures like *The Hebrides*. Schumann's four symphonies are fine broad romantic works in the Beethoven tradition, but it remained for Brahms – hailed by Schumann as 'he who was to come' – to compose what was, perhaps foolishly, hailed as 'Beethoven's tenth'. Much influenced by Brahms, as well as by Czech folk music, Dvořák achieved the Beethovenian total of nine symphonies, as did Gustav Mahler (see page 139), who also left fragments of another which have since been welded into a 'tenth symphony': many of them are on a massive scale and follow the practice established in Beethoven's ninth of using voices as well as instruments.

In the course of the nineteenth century, symphonic music assumed shapes quite different from the symphony as Beethoven left it. Berlioz claimed to 'begin where Beethoven left off' with his 'Fantastic' Symphony, but this feverish piece of programme music, like the introspective symphonies of Tchaikovsky, is far removed from the spirit of Beethoven. Liszt, like Berlioz, wrote programmatic works such as the 'Faust' Symphony; and he also developed the SYMPHONIC POEM, a symphonic work, usually in one movement, with a definite story to tell: *Mazeppa, Hungaria* and *Les Préludes* are among the best known. Smetana, Dvořák, César Franck, Moussorgsky and Sibelius are among the many composers who found the form of the symphonic poem to their liking, as did the most remarkable of Wagner's German successors, Richard Strauss (1864–1949). He produced a series of great tone pictures of Wagnerian proportions such as *Thus Spake Zarathustra* (1896) and *A Hero's Life* (1899), as well as numerous operas, some intensely dramatic, like the early *Electra* and *Salome*, and some romantic to an almost excessive degree, such as *Der Rosenkavalier* and other works that came later in life. For Richard Strauss occupies a place in musical history when the bloom of romanticism is becoming overblown – ripe, in fact, for decay.

Verdi's successor in Italian Opera, Giacomo Puccini (1858–1924), was able to employ the rich palette of late romanticism with a firm hand, and operas such as *La Bohème* (1896), *Tosca* (1900) and *Madam Butterfly* (1904) are among the most effective and appealing ever written. And music in France, too, developed in rather healthier ways than it did in Germany. The work of the Belgian organist César Franck (1822–1890) has a kind of luminous lyricism; that of Gabriel Fauré (1845–1924) is exquisitely wrought; Emmanuel Chabrier (1841–1894) was one of several French composers at this period who produced vigorous 'likeable' music. Camille Saint-Saëns (1835–1921) was perhaps supreme among them – 'the only great composer who is not a genius', as he's been called. But in Claude Debussy (1862–1918), France did produce a genius. His delicate and vivid imagination dispensed with everything that was overdone, creating incisive musical pictures which vibrate in the memory just as surely as the great works of the impressionist painters who were Debussy's contemporaries. Maurice Ravel (1875–1937) was another master who treated the apparatus of romantic music – opera, ballet, the large symphony orchestra – with a new and refreshing astringency.

As for Britain in the nineteenth century, it was, as Mr A. J. B. Hutchings calls it in *The Pelican History of Music*, a 'conservative German colony in the concert room and an Italian one in the theatre'. Notable visitors came in plenty – Wagner, Rossini, Liszt, Verdi, Mendelssohn, among others. Native British music was decorously conformist, though highly accomplished too, in the case, for instance, of Hubert Parry (1848–1918),

The most famous Italian
operatic tenor, Enrico Caruso

Charles Villiers Stanford (1852–1924) and Arthur Sullivan (1842–1900),
who was most disappointed that his serious music carried less weight with
the public than the brilliant light operas he composed in collaboration
with W. S. Gilbert. Not until the production of the 'Enigma' Variations
by Edward Elgar (see page 141) at Düsseldorf in 1899 did a Victorian
British composer make much impact abroad: Elgar was saluted for his
mastery of the orchestra by Richard Strauss, and was more than a match
for him in musical colour and human feeling. Most of Elgar's music is
unmistakably 'English'. So is that of Ralph Vaughan Williams (1872–
1958), who, with a number of other composers, came to maturity in the
early years of the twentieth century. Vaughan Williams spent much time
collecting folk songs and studying British Church music of earlier ages,
influences which are very apparent in the modal flavour of much of his
work. Frederick Delius (1862–1934), born in Bradford of German parents,
was a more cosmopolitan figure. His marvellously atmospheric tone-
poems – *On Hearing the First Cuckoo in Spring, Summer Night on the River* and
others – display the 'sense of flow' Delius believed all-important in music:
there is also a quality of mystical yearning in Delius's music which comes
out very strongly in one of his finest works, *Sea Drift* (composed in 1904),
a setting of words by the American poet Walt Whitman.

Across the Atlantic, as in Britain during much of the nineteenth century,
most art-music and most leading musicians were imported. There was an
opera house in New Orleans as early as 1808, and a French company from
there visited New York in the 1820s. Opera rapidly became more fashionable in New York and other big cities in the fifties and sixties, but almost
all the stars were German or Italian: in fact when the first American

grand opera, William Henry Fry's *Leonore*, was given in New York in 1858, it was sung in Italian. Among the musical celebrities who paid highly successful visits to the States were Dvořák (who came over to lead Mrs Jeanette Thurber's National Conservatory), Offenbach and Johann Strauss: Strauss conducted a vast orchestra advertised to consist of 'one thousand musicians' at the Great National Peace Jubilee, organized by the Irish musical showman Patrick Gilmore (who was also a cornet virtuoso) in 1869. 'Monster' manifestations of this kind were highly popular at this period, and not only in the United States; one has only to think of the vast Crystal Palace erected in Hyde Park, London, for the Great Exhibition of 1851, and the Royal Albert Hall, built in commemoration of Queen Victoria's Prince Consort, though its seven-thousand capacity is dwarfed by many American auditoriums.

If 'serious' music was largely imported, popular music in nineteenth-century America had great vitality – in church and chapel and at revival meetings; in the growth of the band movement inaugurated by the ambitious Patrick Gilmore and crowned by the work of John Philip Sousa, whose band toured all over the United States and remained in being till Sousa's death in 1932; and in the 'nigger minstrel' shows which were the most popular of all forms of entertainment in the latter half of the nineteenth century (Stephen Foster composed his immortal *Old Folks at Home* for the Christy Minstrels).

It was from all the various strands of popular American music that the first really significantly American composer, Charles Ives (see page 143), fashioned his style. He was not content, like his contemporary Edward MacDowell (1861–1908), to take his inspiration from European sources; he turned rather to the town band, the neighbourhood theatre, the chapel and the camp meeting for his ideas, fusing them in compositions which are kaleidoscopic in effect and harmonically very advanced. Ives in fact anticipated the work of Schoenberg in abandoning the traditional key system, as did his contemporary Carl Ruggles (1876–1971). Ives as a creative composer was almost unrecognized in his lifetime, but now we can see him as one of the most individual of all composers and a major pioneer, dismissing what he called the 'Byronic fallacy' of romantic self-expression in favour of an objectivity which is one of the characteristics of music in the twentieth century.

The Music of Modern Man

If it is difficult with any real accuracy to attach labels to the musical movements of the past, it becomes virtually impossible with the music of our own time, for we ourselves are part of the process which produces it. As in the world of politics, there is a questioning of all authority; no single style of composition prevails; and there is a sense of adventure in music which is terrifying to the conservative-minded. These, however, should perhaps remember that many masterpieces were at first greeted with howls of outrage.

From the pioneering work of Charles Ives onwards, America has played a great part in modern music, for not only has the United States (like other American countries) produced important composers of its own, but has attracted such key European-born figures as Béla Bartók (1881–1945), Igor Stravinsky (see page 135), and Paul Hindemith (1895–1953). Arnold Schoenberg (see page 140), though born in Vienna, died in Los Angeles, after spending eight years as Professor of Music at the University of California from 1936 to 1944. The fact that all these influential composers were uprooted from their native soil for part of their lives is perhaps significant in the confused pattern of twentieth-century music.

Schoenberg's earliest works, such as *Transfigured Night*, originally written for string sextet, have the aching sensuality of Wagner and Mahler, but soon he was led, in a dark and determined search for self-integration, to believe that the established key-system was played out. His twelve-tone system and 'tone-row' idea have been of enormous importance in the development of twentieth-century music, but the concept is rarely followed in its entirety by other composers. Schoenberg himself considered his theory was something that should concern only composers; and indeed, as listeners, we feel at first only the dramatic impact of such works as the Violin Concerto, the terrifying concentration-camp story *A Survivor from Warsaw* and the opera *Moses and Aaron*. Schoenberg's outstanding pupil Alban Berg (1885–1935) made some compromises with traditional 'tonality' to produce, among other things, the intensely moving opera *Wozzeck*. Anton Webern (1883–1945) used the twelve-tone system with mathematical precision, treating voices and instruments with the impersonality of science, yet the effect of his work is often hauntingly beautiful, echoing the reverberations of the Balinese gamelan.

An impersonal quality also runs through the many kinds of music written by Igor Stravinsky. He started by inheriting the highly coloured 'barbarity' of older Russian composers, and put it to revolutionary use in his ballet score for Diaghilev, *The Rite of Spring* (1913): its primeval rhythms overthrew romantic delicacy in favour of primitive savagery.

Primitive too were the origins of jazz, born in the Southern States of America out of Negro work-songs, hymns, band-marches, Caribbean and Latin-American rhythms and a hotch-potch of other influences. The forms of jazz varied greatly, from the often deeply emotional 'blues' to slick, syncopated dance music, always with a big element of improvisation. Until the 1890s jazz was mainly confined to the South, and was associated above all with the sleazier night-spots of New Orleans; but then, with the work of Scott Joplin and others, the piano-rag was born, adopting some of the springing rhythm of jazz and leading to the tremendous craze for 'ragtime'. The jazz band as such was first imported into Chicago from the South in 1914 – and the 'Jazz Age' of the twenties and thirties was on its way, with its intoxicating rhythms, raucous instruments, and strident voices, yet also with sharp feeling, brilliant musicianship and, sometimes, extreme sophistication.

The Count Basie orchestra in rehearsal

Jazz is woven into the fabric of much twentieth-century popular music, and has had an immense influence, too, on the art-music scene. Stravinsky was one of the first, and one of the most influential, composers to react. His *Ragtime for Eleven Instruments* and *The Soldier's Tale* are among his many attractive works which owe a great deal to jazz, though in fact it was not until after the Second World War that Stravinsky made his home in the United States. Meanwhile, he had made a return to what he considered the impersonal style of classical and pre-classical music, with such works as *Oedipus Rex* (1927) and the *Symphony of Psalms* (1930), and in later life he adopted the Schoenbergian twelve-tone outlook for a number of short, controversial abstract works, which some considered his finest until then, and others as no more than signposts to a dead end.

The German composer Hindemith, who was Professor of Music at Yale University from 1940 to 1953, was also much influenced by jazz in the 1920s, but later looked to the spirit of Bach in his search for an 'impersonal', strictly musical style, expressing his theories in a series of fugues and interludes for piano called *Ludus Tonalis*, which reflects the pattern of Bach's Forty-eight Preludes and Fugues.

The Hungarian composer Béla Bartók, like his contemporary Zoltán Kodály (1882–1967) found his own identity through a search for the soul of Hungary in her folk music. A passionate libertarian, Bartók said he only felt fully at home in the company of peasants, and he felt a peasant's scepticism about all forms of authority. Dissonant and harsh though some of his music is, he was more strongly influenced by sonata-form than his major contemporaries, and his six string quartets, tense, dramatic, lyrical works, are in the direct tradition of Beethoven. Bartók's last years in the United States were very difficult, though Koussevitzky commissioned one of his major works, the *Concerto for Orchestra*, for the Boston Symphony Orchestra, and there were a few other important concerts. He died at the very moment when his greatness was being generally recognized.

Another very important European expatriate was Edgar Varèse (1885–1965). He rejected the whole idea of music as psychological drama, the conflicts and resolutions of sonata-form, and indeed the concept of harmony itself; instead he concentrated on sounds and noises produced 'accidentally' and spontaneously. His works bring together a variety of rhythms and timbres, the only unifying concept being a sense of the 'opening of space'. The aim is to remove the self from the centre of the picture, to induce in fact a mystical, timeless feeling of contemplation. The spiritual ancestors of Varèse belong, in fact, to the East rather than the West. The same may perhaps be said of John Cage (b. 1912), who sees magic as an agent of spiritual healing, and perhaps for this reason treats silence as a kind of music. He is probably most famous for his 'prepared pianos' – pianos with many sorts of objects added to the strings, such as nuts and bolts, rubber bands and hairpins, and with the pitch of certain strings altered. New and unexpected sounds are thus produced; whether they are interesting or not is a matter of opinion.

John Tilbury with a prepared piano

Very much more accessible is the music of Aaron Copland (b. 1900), who began with a period of academic modern-European experiment, but drew on the background of American folk music for attractive scores such as *Appalachian Spring, Billy the Kid* and *El Salón Mexico*. Virgil Thomson (b. 1896) is another composer who has made use of many kinds of popular American musical idioms in his work. His opera *Four Saints in Three Acts* first won him fame, and another fine achievement is the film score for Robert Flaherty's *Louisiana Story*. Thomson in fact is one of a number of American composers to bridge the gap between 'serious' and popular music in the twentieth century. Another was George Gershwin (1898–1937), who sought to bring Tin Pan Alley into the concert hall with the *Rhapsody in Blue, An American in Paris* and the Piano Concerto, and composed the deeply moving Negro opera *Porgy and Bess*. Gian-Carlo Menotti (b. 1911) used the rather facile romanticism of the Hollywood film score to produce operas like *The Consul* and *The Medium*, highly effective stage works with a sharp contemporary feel, but lacking the edge and urgency of *West Side Story* by Leonard Bernstein (b. 1918). Bernstein, like André Previn (b. 1929) one of the outstanding all-round musicians of our day, seems to be at home in all areas of music, and in his very remarkable *Mass* he makes use of them all.

But America is more than the United States, and the twentieth century has seen the growth of national groups of important composers in other countries. Outstanding perhaps was Heitor Villa-Lobos of Brazil (1887–1959), whose vast output exploits the exotic variety of Brazilian folk and popular music, combining it in the *Bachianas Brasileiras* with the disciplines of Bach. Carlos Chávez (b. 1899) has explored the resources of Mexican music in a similar way, while Alberto Ginastera (b. 1916) is one of the outstanding Argentinian composers of our time.

In Europe, as in America, music has developed in the twentieth century in a great variety of ways, from far-out experiment to traditional forms. With the exception of Soviet Russia, where composers must exert a conservative control over their material, there has been a general trend away from Western romantic striving and towards the more contemplative attitudes of the East.

Although Ernest Bloch (1880–1959) lived in the United States from 1924, his music is fundamentally the expression of the alienated Jewish community which has suffered so appallingly in the Europe of our century, but there is a sense of almost Asiatic resignation in the deeply moving *Schelomo* and the *Sacred Service*. We have already mentioned the gamelan effect of Webern's sonorities: his mathematical approach to music was inherited by Karlheinz Stockhausen (b. 1928), much of whose work is so intricate that it can only be performed electronically. He has also experimented with 'controlled improvisation', in which the performers are encouraged to play different sections of Stockhausen scores either separately or together, in whatever order they choose. The idea is that something new and exciting may be accidentally created in such 'happenings'. Eastern influences are also at work in the music of another German composer, Carl Orff (b. 1895) in such pieces as *Aphrodite*, but Orff has won a great degree of popular success with compositions like *Carmina Burana*, a reworking of the bawdy musical material which flourished in medieval times alongside monasticism and provided relief from religious vocation.

Religious devotion lies at the heart of the work of the French composer Olivier Messiaen (b. 1908), one of whose most important works is the piano composition *Vingts Regards sur l'Enfant Jésus* (literally 'Twenty Looks at the Infant Jesus'). The looks are long and contemplative, again in the timeless oriental manner, making use of a slow, shimmering texture of sound. Like Messiaen, Pierre Boulez (b. 1925) has blended the style of Indian ragas and talas with the twelve-tone technique. His many works, of which *Le Marteau sans Maître* ('The Hammer without a Master') is an important example, are rich in multitudinous sonorities; the purpose, again, is mystical – to explore hidden areas of awareness. The important Italian composer Luigi Dallapiccola (b. 1904) treats Christian religious themes in a style which effectively combines Schoenbergian practice with the great Italian tradition of vocal music.

Two members of the French group known as 'Les Six' which, in Paris in the years immediately after the First World War, cultivated a kind of ironic simplicity, went on to compose major religious works: the Swiss Arthur Honegger (1892–1955) and Francis Poulenc (1899–1963), whose piquant harmony adds a little spice to the general sweetness of his musical manner. In Poland, Karol Szymanowski (1883–1937) and the experimental Witold Lutoslawski (b. 1913) have both made it their business to compose large-scale religious works, as part of a widespread concern to rediscover, beyond the acute divisions and tensions of everyday modern life, a much-needed healing unity.

Russia has always stood somewhat apart from European musical developments, and in the twentieth century has continued to do so. In the Soviet Union, of course, the State religion is Communism, and many have been the works composed to glorify it. Sometimes fine Soviet composers have genuinely been able to identify themselves with the theme of the brotherhood of man in the Socialist State, and have produced splendid patriotic music. But State direction of their work has cost many composers intense inner suffering. Prominent among such composers was Serge Prokofiev (1891–1953). With 'Les Six' in the Paris of the twenties, he developed a satirical gift which later in life was not always appreciated by the authorities. He was criticized for being a decadent bourgeois, and during long periods he lived in Russia in a kind of spiritual banishment. Yet his profound patriotism cannot possibly be in doubt when we hear, for example, his magnificent opera *War and Peace*. Dmitri Shostakovich (b. 1906) has also had his difficulties with the Kremlin, and some of his works, it's thought, contain a kind of cryptic autobiography which hints at his sufferings. But there is an affirmation of hope for the human spirit

Jacqueline du Pré and orchestra, conducted by Daniel Barenboim

in most of his major works, and this finds acceptance with the authorities as being in key with the onward surge of Communism.

Great Britain, too, like Russia, has historically stood somewhat apart from the mainstream musical developments of continental Europe, and in general has somewhat lagged behind. Thus the English nationalism of Vaughan Williams and Gustav Holst (1874–1934) came a good deal later than the parallel movement elsewhere. The deeply religious composer Edmund Rubbra (b. 1901) has founded his large output of symphonic and choral music very much on the English tradition. So, to a certain extent, has William Walton (b. 1902). Like Elgar, he has produced some very stirring patriotic and ceremonial music; there is also the glittering splendour of his oratorio *Belshazzar's Feast*. But wit predominates in the early *Façade*, and there is much nostalgic beauty in such works as the viola and violin concertos. Michael Tippett (b. 1905) is a long way from the civilized detachment which is one of the characteristics of Walton. His great oratorio *A Child of Our Time* deals most movingly with twentieth-century persecution, and in his operas, especially *The Midsummer Marriage*, Tippett is concerned with ancient pre-Christian rituals which relate to the human soul at a deep and primitive level.

One of the most remarkable composers of the twentieth century is Benjamin Britten (b. 1913). In the view of his many admirers, Britten can be compared to Mozart, in that his music speaks directly to his hearers, while at the same time making few easy concessions to popular taste. Britten is clearly aware of all kinds of music, Eastern and Western, ancient and modern, and borrows from each the elements he needs for each particular task. English influences – the Anglican Church tradition, the music of Purcell – are strong, and there is a powerful feel of the English east coast, where Britten lives, in much of his music, especially in his first major opera (which some think his best), *Peter Grimes*. Like many of Britten's works, *Grimes* is concerned with the victimization of the odd-man-out by a relentlessly conventional society. The *War Requiem* presents in starkly contemporary terms the contrasted forces of terror and of pity, and looks for a resolution in other-wordly innocence. And Britten's *A Midsummer Night's Dream*, like Tippett's *Midsummer Marriage*, looks through the apparent realities of everyday life to the magical mysteries beyond.

Much more than we have space to mention goes on in the world of creative music today. In this brief historical survey we have included just a few of the outstanding characters and characteristics of music down the ages, and have moreover kept to 'art music'. We have scarcely touched on the continual stream of folk music which wells up wherever in the world there is a heart with feelings that (to adapt a famous phrase of Wordsworth's) lie too deep for words.

Benjamin Britten

9
A Gallery of Great Composers

Henry Purcell (1658?–1695)

So little is known about the life of Purcell that until recently it was un-certain which of two brothers was the composer's father. Now we know that Henry was the son of Thomas Purcell, a Gentleman of the Chapel Royal and capable all-round musician, who very naturally secured a place for the boy as a Chorister of the Chapel Royal as soon as he showed signs of talent. John Blow gave him some instruction in composition, and at the age of fourteen Henry Purcell composed an *Address of the Children of the Chapel Royal to the King*. His musical abilities must have developed rapidly in every way, for at about the age of twenty he replaced Blow as organist of Westminster Abbey. By a strange turn of fate, Blow resumed the office after Purcell's early death.

Purcell composed some fine instrumental music: fantasias for strings which traced their ancestry back to the style of the late Elizabethan Age, and 'sonnatas' for two violins, cello and harpsichord which were claimed to be a 'just imitation of the most fam'd Italian masters' but in fact were a great deal better than imitations. The composer's greatest achievements, however, were in vocal music, which might perhaps be expected from one who began life as a singer and is said to have possessed as an adult a remarkably agile counter-tenor voice.

From about 1680 he began writing a long series of 'welcome-songs' and odes, many of them superb, for ceremonial occasions, and composi-tions for the theatre. Generally speaking he was called upon to provide incidental music for plays which sometimes – as in *Diocletian*, adapted from a piece by Beaumont and Fletcher – expanded into a whole act of song and dance in the manner of the court masque. Some of the numbers Purcell wrote for these plays rank among his finest pieces: examples are 'What Shall I Do to Show How Much I Love Her?' from *Diocletian*, the frost scene from *King Arthur* and numerous passages from *The Faerie Queene*, an adaptation of Shakespeare's *A Midsummer Night's Dream*. Only once did Purcell have the chance to write a complete opera, when Mr Josias Priest commissioned *Dido and Aeneas* for his boarding school at Chelsea; and Purcell took full advantage of the chance, producing a work which holds the stage well in our own time with its deeply felt and dramatic music. *Dido* was a historic departure in Purcell's day, for, in most of the entertainments of the period, music was just one of many ingredients, thought to be no more important than the 'machines' which produced spectacular transformation scenes, or the highly elaborate costumes. Purcell aimed at a truer kind of expression in his opera (which he described neatly in the preface as a 'story sung with proper action') and in several scenes, notably perhaps Dido's great lament 'When I am Laid in Earth', created unforgettable music.

Johann Sebastian Bach (1685–1750)

'Music owes as much to Johann Sebastian Bach', wrote Robert Schumann, 'as Christianity does to its founder.' The words of a fanatical admirer, who, along with Mendelssohn, began to realize the importance of Bach almost a century after his death. In his own day, Bach was renowned throughout Germany as a great keyboard player and admired by a few discerning spirits for his compositions, but it has only been in the last hundred years that he has taken his place with Handel, his exact contemporary, at the forefront of Baroque music and, some would say, as the greatest of all composers.

Born in the little town of Eisenach, Johann Sebastian belonged to a family of able musicians. Before he was ten, both his father and mother died, and the boy went to live with his elder brother, who punished him, we are told, for copying out by moonlight the manuscripts he found in the music cupboard. He went to school for three years at Lüneburg near Hamburg, and at the age of eighteen was appointed organist at Arnstadt, not far from his home town. Probably the most famous episode of this period is Bach's journey of three hundred miles on foot to hear the great Danish organist Buxtehude at Lübeck. The four-week period of leave he had been granted somehow extended itself to four months, and Bach got into trouble with the authorities – not for the last time: throughout his career he considered the demands of his art paramount, and would submit to no questioning of his judgment on the subject, no matter whence it came. While he was at Arnstadt, Bach married his second cousin Maria Barbara, who was to bear the first seven of Bach's twenty children.

In Bach's day a musician looked for his livelihood either to the Church or to some noble patron, and Johann Sebastian's versatile genius fitted him for either kind of work; in later life, the emphasis was to fall on Church music, but in his twenties and thirties Bach was in the service of noblemen. This, of course, involved producing a good deal of vocal music for the Chapel, but instrumental music, too, was in demand. During his years of service from 1708 to 1717 with the Duke of Saxe-Weimar, Bach wrote many fine organ works as well as some two hundred Church cantatas, and at Cöthen (where he was Capellmeister – that is Director of Music, in the Chapel and outside it – to Prince Leopold of Anhalt-Cöthen from 1717 to 1723) he was required to produce instrumental works of many kinds, among them the six great 'Brandenburg' Concertos, written at the request of the Margrave of Brandenburg. While he was at Cöthen, Bach's first wife died, and eighteen months later he married Anna Magdalena Wilcke, who gave birth to thirteen children, of whom six survived infancy. However, she found time to take keyboard lessons from

Dance drama in *West Side Story*

her husband, and the little pieces of the 'Anna Magdalena' notebooks are still studied by budding pianists. Three of the Bach children, Wilhelm Friedemann, Carl Philipp Emanuel and Johann Christian were to become internationally famous musicians in their own right, and for them, too, Bach wrote special exercises, heading the ones destined for Wilhelm Friedemann 'In the name of Jesus'. That was the spirit in which Bach sought to conduct his life, for he was a devout, untroubled Christian, and his noblest achievements were works written to the glory of God.

In 1722 Bach applied for the post of Cantor (which combined the teaching of Latin with the training of choirboys) at St Thomas's School in Leipzig, and it was for this school that he wrote the first of his great 'passions', *The Passion According to St John*. However, it was only after his rivals Telemann and Christoph Graupner had turned the job down that Bach was offered the post, and the grudging manner of his appointment set the keynote for twenty-seven years of intermittent friction between Bach and the municipal authorities. Bach suffered as schoolmaster and choirmaster from the fact he was no disciplinarian; moreover the forces at his disposal for his great Church compositions were generally inadequate, and his music was often misunderstood. 'What does this mean?' asked an outraged noble lady at a performance of one of Bach's passions – 'God help us, if it is not for certain an opera-comedy!' For all his versatility, Bach never did write an opera; but perhaps the lady had a point, for in his great religious works – the *St John Passion* and *St Matthew Passion*, the Christmas and Easter Oratorios, the *B Minor Mass* and hundreds of cantatas – Bach showed his profound instinct for drama.

It is unlikely that Bach heard adequate performances of any of his works which he was not able to perform himself at the keyboard of organ or clavichord. For these instruments, he composed a great deal of magnificent music, including the famous *Forty-eight Preludes and Fugues*, great numbers of fantasias, fugues and 'Chorale Preludes' (derived from the improvisations required of the organist in the Lutheran service), the *Goldberg Variations* and the loftily intellectual *Art of Fugue*. But something more than music's most brilliant brain was required to represent adequately the themes of Christianity: Bach poured into these works a deeply feeling soul, conveying his meaning with such force to future generations that Mendelssohn, after playing one of Bach's choral preludes, remarked to Schumann, 'If I had lost all my religious faith, this thing alone would be sufficient to restore it.'

But all this wealth of feeling by-passed the burghers of Leipzig. When Bach died, blind, at the age of sixty-five, the town council, appointing his successor, expressed no regret. His widow was buried in a pauper's grave. A few enthusiasts went on teaching Bach's music in Berlin; Mozart admired it and preached the Bach gospel in Vienna. Then a teacher called Carl Zelter aroused the enthusiasm of Felix Mendelssohn, and through him, at last, the world began to learn the true stature of the Cantor of St Thomas's School.

A scene from Mozart's opera *Così Fan Tutte*

Henry Purcell   Johann Sebastian Bach

George Frederic Handel (1685–1759)

About a month before Bach was born, his great musical 'twin' Handel first saw the light of day in Halle. Though there has been a tendency to bracket them together, the two men were very different in professional approach and temperament. Bach's life was lived against the domestic background of a family man, in his native Germany; Handel, a lifelong bachelor, was adventurous, travelling widely in the musical world. Bach wrote no operas, Handel composed dozens. One thing they had in common, perhaps, was that their most memorable achievements were in oratorio, though Handel turned to that medium only when his operas lost favour.

Handel's father, a respected barber-surgeon, was against a musical career for his son, but allowed him to display his exceptional talent as a boy of eleven at the court of the Electress Sophia Charlotte in Berlin. Not long after this episode, Handel senior died, and George Frederic abandoned his law studies as soon as he could. At seventeen he became organist of Halle Cathedral; at eighteen he left home to seek success in Hamburg, famed for its opera, and succeeded in getting his first two operatic efforts staged before he was twenty-one. Then, on the strength of a single introduction, he set off for Italy, home of everything then thought worthwhile in the world of opera. Florence, Rome and Naples contributed to his store of experience, and in Venice Handel won great acclaim with his opera *Agrippina*, which led to his being offered the post of Capellmeister to Prince Ernest of Hanover at the early age of twenty-five.

However, Handel was still restless and soon obtained leave to visit England, where, in February 1711, his opera *Rinaldo* scored an immediate hit. After another few months in Hanover and a short visit to his home in Halle, he returned to London and remained there for the rest of his life, apart from short trips abroad. He had already accepted an allowance from Queen Anne before being released from his duties in Hanover, so there could have been some embarrassment when in 1714 that lady died and Handel's Hanoverian master became King of England; but pride in the achievements of his former protégé softened the King's resentment, and he was soon to be seen, with his mistresses, at Handel's operas.

For a time Handel acted as Capellmeister to the Duke of Chandos, who lived in state at his great new house 'Cannons', near Edgware, north of London, and for him he composed ceremonial anthems and instrumental music; but Handel's main preoccupation was with opera. The Italian fashion prevailed, and Handel was suited by training and talent to comply with it; but he had to operate in a London riddled with sharp rivalries and slander, and to cope not only with the tantrums of his star singers, imported at immense cost from Italy, but with the intrigues of powerful opponents. At one moment, Handel was the universal hero, courted and admired by all; at the next he was vilified as yet another German immigrant, no more welcome than the unattractive members of the Hanoverian royal house. His fortunes rose and fell over and over again, and since he himself was involved in theatrical management, his financial fortunes too were extremely unsteady. But he was enormously determined; and when an opera failed, and one of his rivals triumphed for a time, Handel was almost always able to come back with a new work, or a novel singer, to win once again the plaudits of the Town. He survived the stinging satire of John Gay's *The Beggar's Opera* (1728), but not long afterwards, sensing a public weariness with Italian opera, he began to compose his long series of English oratorios on religious subjects – *Esther, Saul, Israel in Egypt, Samson, Solomon* and *Jephtha* are among them – which were sung, instead of opera, in the theatres. Bishops fulminated at these impious proceedings, but the boxes were subscribed for, and the pit was packed. But still he was at the mercy of the fickle public; once he came very near to being imprisoned for debt, and in 1741 he withdrew totally for a time from public life.

In those few months at home in Brook Street he worked feverishly: in twenty-four days he committed to paper one of the world's supreme works of art, the oratorio *Messiah*. When food was brought to him, he left it uneaten; and to the servant who found him in tears after completing the 'Hallelujah Chrous', Handel said, 'I did think I did see all Heaven before me, and the great God himself.' Dublin had the honour of hearing the first performance, for London at that moment had tired of Handel; *Messiah* was given in Neal's Music Hall in the Irish capital in April 1742.

Encouraged, Handel returned to London, but his struggles were not over. Hampered by increasing ill-health, he continued to work hard, turning out eight more superb oratorios after *Messiah*, most of them put on with great success at Covent Garden or the King's Theatre in the Haymarket, where they would run, rather like operas, for as many performances as the demand would stand. There was other work too: the tutelage of royal children, and commissions of one kind or another for royal occasions.

George Frederic Handel   Joseph Haydn

In the final phase of Handel's life, when he had become almost totally blind, the English at last recognized the towering genius of the lonely irascible old man who had chosen to become one of them; and when he died, at the age of seventy-four, it was to Westminster Abbey that they carried him for burial. Of his musical genius, what is there to add to the words of the dying Beethoven, who pointed to his collection of Handel's works and said, 'There lies the truth'?

Joseph Haydn (1732–1809)

During his long life Haydn was responsible for great changes in the art of music; and he had the gratification, denied to so many musicians, of being recognized in his lifetime for the great composer he was.

It had not always been so. Haydn was born into a poor family in the village of Rohrau on the borders of Austria and Hungary, and even though, as Haydn wrote later, he got 'more thrashings than food in the process', he was lucky to be patronized by the headmaster of a school in the local town of Hainburg, where he was recruited at the age of eight for the famous Vienna Boys' Choir. He was a mischievous lad, and when he went so far as to cut off the pigtail of another boy during choir practice, the choirmaster was delighted to see the back of him. Haydn was seventeen and completely penniless.

By great good fortune he met a friend of his father's who made him a small loan (later scrupulously repaid), and Haydn set himself up in a decrepit attic with a 'worm-eaten' harpsichord on which he studied the works of C.P.E. Bach; he also gave a few lessons and picked up freelance jobs as a violinist. Luck was with him again when he met the Italian singing master Nicolò Porpora, and became his accompanist, thus gaining the chance to be spotted by one of the wealthy patrons who were the only means at that time by which a musician could hope to attain a steady living. When he was twenty-eight, Haydn became Capellmeister to a Bohemian noble, and on the strength of this new-found security got married to Maria Keller, the sister of a girl he really loved who became a nun: Maria had no understanding of him or his work, and the marriage was most unhappy.

When he was twenty-nine, Haydn was offered the job of Assistant Capellmeister by one of the wealthiest noblemen in Europe, Prince Paul Anton Esterhazy; and Haydn was to spend most of the rest of his working life in the service of the Esterhazy family, first at Eisenstadt, and later at the vast new Palace of Esterház, in a remote part of Hungary. The family, particularly in the days of Prince Nikoláus, when Haydn had become Capellmeister, were (in Haydn's view) far too fond of this marshy place miles from civilization, and, in the autumn of 1772 he composed the famous 'Farewell' Symphony, at the end of which the musicians of the orchestra got up and left the platform one by one, snuffing their candles as they went – a hint to the great man that it was high time to set off for Christmas in Vienna.

Yet the isolation of Esterház was the composer's opportunity. He had a good orchestra, facilities which included an opera house and a marionette theatre, and a patron who passionately admired his work. Haydn recognized his good fortune: 'Not only did I have the encourage-ment of constant approval, but as conductor of the orchestra, I could experiment. Cut off from the world, I had no one to bother me and I was forced to become original.'

Into his orchestral symphonies Haydn poured a quite new kind of strength; this hitherto polite form of music-making became positively tragic in such symphonies as No. 26, the 'Lamentation', and No. 44, the 'Mourning' Symphony. In Haydn's hands, the string quartet became a carefully wrought dialogue for four equally important voices; and in the numerous operas Haydn was required to produce, he avoided the worst artificialities of the Italian style, choosing one subject, *Il Mondo della Luna* ('The World of the Moon'), which was strangely prophetic and has enjoyed a number of Space Age revivals. Haydn also wrote a number of works for the marionette theatre; indeed, as his importance in the house-hold grew, he kept such a theatre himself.

In his fifties, Haydn was in a position to negotiate with publishers and accept commissions from abroad; at this period of his life, too, he struck up a close personal friendship with the young Mozart, whom he greatly admired. Then, in 1790, Prince Nikolaus died, and with him the Esterhazy interest in music. Haydn was free to accept the invitation of the concert promoter Johann Peter Salomon to come to London, and the English capital was the scene of many of Haydn's greatest public triumphs, during two prolonged visits, between 1791 and 1795. There, the twelve magnificent 'Salomon' symphonies were written and per-formed, Haydn was lionized everywhere he went, and the King offered him an apartment in Windsor Castle in an attempt to persuade him to stay in Britain.

But there had been another change in the Esterhazy family: music was to be restored to its former importance, and Haydn, now rich and famous, returned to Vienna. For the Esterhazys he composed six great Masses, including the so-called 'Nelson' Mass (Nelson and Haydn met and exchanged keepsakes); and at this period Haydn also produced two other great choral works, *The Creation* and *The Seasons*, both enormously successful, and both giving Haydn a chance to express the intense feeling for nature which can so often be sensed in his music and perhaps had its origins in his country childhood.

Haydn's deep religious feelings produced in him a carefree confidence in God, and it is clear that he must have been a most attractive character. He achieved worldly success, but never at the expense of his natural honesty and good sense. Asked what lessons there were in his career for youth, he replied, 'Young people can learn from my example that something can come out of nothing. What I have become is all the result of dire need.'

Wolfgang Amadeus Mozart (1756–1791)

Mozart, probably, is the musician most admired by other musicians. Chopin's dying words are said to have been 'Play Mozart in memory of me', and Tchaikovsky decided to devote himself to music as a result of seeing a performance of Mozart's opera *Don Giovanni* when he was twelve years old. But Tchaikovsky also felt that Mozart's music was 'full of *unapproachable*, divine beauty', and perhaps many newcomers to his music share that feeling.

If you come to music first through the great romantics, and are swept off your feet by their swirling floods of sound (as for example in the Fourth, Fifth and Sixth symphonies of Tchaikovsky himself), then Mozart may sound rather thin to you at first. This is because he expressed himself within the musical conventions of his own time: you begin to recognize his genius when you notice how extraordinarily resourceful and varied he is in the way he uses those conventions, and how much human feeling underlies the unfailing elegance of his music.

Intensely dramatic are some of the scenes in his opera *Don Giovanni*, which tells the story of Don Juan: an instance is when one of his girlfriends, Donna Anna, recognizes him as the murderer of her father. It was her outburst of rage and pride which above all impressed Tchaikovsky as a boy: 'I trembled with horror; I longed to shout, to weep, to groan, crushed by the violence of my impression.' There is another spine-chilling moment in *Don Giovanni* when the ghostly statue of Donna Anna's father comes to life and takes revenge, sending the Don's soul to hell, escorted by fiery demons: all this is marvellously expressed in Mozart's music, with no more than the addition of trombones to the normal orchestra of his day.

However intense the emotion expressed in Mozart's music, it is always well-mannered, which removes it a long way from the soul-searchings of the romantics, who elaborate on every detail of their own inner sufferings. You may find an echo of your own feelings in their work, in which case you will respond strongly to it; but there may come a moment when you think 'I don't really want to hear all the gory details of So-and-So's operation yet again', and at that moment you are probably ready to listen to Mozart. He was not concerned with his own sufferings (though they were often great) but simply with giving pleasure to others through the medium of his chosen art. 'In music', wrote Mozart, 'the passions, whether violent or not, should never be so expressed as to reach the point of causing disgust; and music, even in situations of the greatest horror, should never be painful to the ear, but should flatter and charm it, and thereby always remains music.'

So far we have spoken of the expression of intense feeling in Mozart's music, because superficial listeners sometimes miss this quality. What is much more obvious is Mozart's high-spirited wit: you will find it bubbling out exuberantly in many of his concert pieces, but above all in the comic moments from Mozart's operas – and there are plenty of them. Even in *Don Giovanni*, the drama is relieved when the Don's servant Leporello, in the famous 'catalogue' song, lists his master's conquests over the fair sex, numerous in every country, but in Spain no fewer than a thousand and three.

If you are approaching Mozart for the first time, try listening to his last two symphonies: No. 40 in G minor – whose opening theme became Top of the Pops as 'Mozart 40' because here the tension and excitement are very apparent within the firm classical framework – and No. 41 in C (the 'Jupiter'). If you play the piano, there are duet arrangements of these and other Mozart symphonies which are fun to attempt. If you have the chance, go and see *The Marriage of Figaro*, *Don Giovanni* or *Così Fan Tutte*, which roughly means 'All Women Are Like That' and is a very amusing story about a couple of soldiers who disguise themselves as Albanians to test the fidelity of their sweethearts. After that there is a whole world of Mozart to explore: concertos for piano, violin and numerous other instruments; religious music (try the beautiful *Ave Verum Corpus*, or *Laudate Dominum*); sonatas of many kinds, chamber music, songs. And do read Mozart's letters: full of humour, they vividly describe the life of a musician in the eighteenth century. You will read how Mozart and his sister as brilliant children were paraded round Europe like circus animals by their father: how the young Wolfgang returned later with his mother to Paris, where his mother died in poverty and the wealthy patrons who had doted on Wolfgang as a child were no longer interested. For a time Mozart was employed by the Archbishop of Salzburg, and in a letter home he neatly summed up the social position of the composer at that time. 'We lunch at twelve o'clock,' he wrote. 'Our party consists of the two valets, the controller, the confectioner, the two cooks and – my insignificant self. By the way, the valets sit at the top of the table. I have the honour of being placed above the cooks.'

Ludwig Van Beethoven (1770–1827)

With Beethoven, music breaks out from the eighteenth century into a new kind of freedom. It is highly significant that for his only opera, *Fidelio*,

Wolfgang Amadeus Mozart   Ludwig Van Beethoven

Beethoven chose a plot concerning a political prisoner, and that one of the most moving moments in that great work occurs when the inmates of the prison are released briefly into the sunshine.

Like Mozart, Beethoven had aristocratic patrons, but he refused to treat them as superiors. There's a famous story of how Beethoven and the poet Goethe, on a walk together, encountered the Royal Court walking towards them. 'Keep your arm linked in mine – they must make room for us, not we for them,' said Beethoven. Goethe withdrew his arm to bow deeply as the Empress passed, but Beethoven marched straight through the courtiers with the barest nod and then halted for his friend to catch up. 'I have waited for you,' he said, 'because I honour and revere you as you deserve; but you have done too much honour to these others.'

Beethoven deeply sympathized with the 'Liberty, Equality and Fraternity' ideals of the French Revolution, dedicating his Third, the 'Heroic', Symphony to Napoleon, whom he regarded at first as a liberator of mankind. But the moment he heard that Napoleon had declared himself Emperor, he tore out the title-page of the score with the words 'Now he will tread under foot all the rights of man, indulge only his ambition, become a tyrant.' Thereafter his sympathies lay with the British and their allies in their long war against the French dictator, vividly describing part of the struggle in his 'Battle' Symphony and writing variations on 'Rule Britannia' and the British national anthem, which incidentally he greatly admired. To the credit of Britain, the Royal Philharmonic Society was quick to realize Beethoven's genius, sending him a present of £100 when he was dying, which touched the great man profoundly. He himself presented the Society with one of his greatest masterpieces, the 'Choral' Symphony.

Beethoven's stature was in fact recognized widely in his lifetime. As a young man he was a brilliant virtuoso pianist, and right through his life he continued to command something like homage from fashionable

Vienna: this in spite of the fact that as time went on he became, it seemed, increasingly hostile and boorish in manner, living alone in a squalor that could only be faced by his most admiring visitors. What made this brilliant man, who might have enjoyed all the rewards of fame, turn almost savagely against society, and retreat into the recesses of his own soul? It can be summed up in one word – deafness.

In the summer of 1802, when he was only just over thirty years old, he described his inmost feelings in a kind of confession known as the *Heiligenstadt Testament*:

> O you men who believe that I am malevolent, stubborn or misanthropic, how greatly you wrong me! You do not know the secret cause behind the appearance: for six years I have been suffering an incurable affliction, and I was compelled early in my life to isolate myself, for I could not bring myself to say to men: 'Speak louder, shout, for I am deaf!' How could I admit to being defective in that very sense which should be more highly developed in me than in other men? Oh, I cannot do it. Therefore you must forgive me if you see me draw back when I would gladly mingle with you.

Beethoven tells us that only the thought of his art prevented him from committing suicide, the feeling that he had to go on enduring 'this wretched existence' for the sake of what he knew he had to give the world.

And so Beethoven lived the rest of his life as a prisoner, condemned to the solitary confinement of deafness. But, to quote the composer's own words again, 'Artists are fiery, they do not weep'; and we can often hear, in the titanic power of Beethoven's works, how he literally hammered his way out of his invisible cell to make contact with the rest of mankind. Listen to the discordant clamour which heralds the 'Ode to Joy' at the end of the Ninth Symphony, when Beethoven seems to be shouting '*Listen* to me, world – what I have to say to you now you *must* hear.' Or listen to the mighty opening of the 'Hammerklavier' Sonata, which seems to burst out from the confines of a mere piano with irresistible force. This assertive, death-defying Beethoven is a very great and inspiring composer.

But there is another Beethoven who is greater still. If it had not been for the tragedy of his deafness, would he have been led to discover within himself the uncanny serenity which lies at the heart of his finest music? In the centre of terrible storms, sailors say there is a place of peace, and Beethoven found his way to such a place, especially towards the end of his life. You will sense it in the slow movement of the 'Hammerklavier' Sonata and in other late piano sonatas, in the Adagio of the Ninth Symphony, and above all in the later string quartets, which many people think the most profoundly spiritual music ever written.

But this Beethoven is not, at first, easily accessible. People come to it by degrees. Enough at first if you can enjoy the untroubled lyricism of the first movement of the so-called 'Moonlight' Sonata, the melody at the heart of the 'Pathétique' Sonata: from there you may go to the drama of the Fifth Symphony and be led to sample the glories of the nine symphonies in general. But don't pass by the very appealing 'Kreutzer' and 'Spring' violin sonatas, or miss the glorious 'Archduke Trio'. By such routes you may be led to try the mighty *Mass in D*, and ultimately to follow Beethoven through his bitterest struggles to the 'peace which passeth all understanding' expressed in the profoundest works of this noble man.

Franz Schubert (1797–1828)

In the brief thirty-one years of his life, Schubert became one of the most endearing characters in music history. A bespectacled, somewhat tubby figure, only 4 feet 11 inches tall, caring little for reward, he poured out music with a prodigality which matched his warm-hearted nature. 'What I feel in my heart,' he once said, 'I give to the world.'

As if aware that he had little time to spare, his genius flowered early. At sixteen he wrote his first symphony, as a farewell gesture to the seminary where he was educated; in the year of his eighteenth birthday, he composed no fewer than one hundred and forty-five songs, the magnificently dramatic *Erl King* among them.

Like Beethoven, and with less soul-searching, Schubert loved the world of nature. On a June day in 1816, he noted: 'There can scarcely be anything more agreeable than to enjoy the green country on an evening after a hot summer day . . . in the uncertain twilight, my heart warmed within me. "How beautiful!" I thought, and stood in silent delight.' This vivid awareness of country sights and sounds finds expression in much of Schubert's music; the song cycle *Die Schöne Müllerin* ('The Miller's Beautiful Daughter') is but one example. And Schubert loved to go off on walking tours with his close friends, when long days in the open air would be rounded off with musical evenings at an inn or some hospitable private house. More often than not it was Schubert's own music that was played or sung, with Schubert at the piano, always ready to improvise dance music for the assembled company.

At home in Vienna, too, such convivial gatherings were the outlet for much of Schubert's finest music, since it was perhaps in his hundreds of wonderfully expressive songs, and in his chamber music, that Schubert most clearly expressed what he felt in his heart. This is not to deny that Schubert's compositions on a larger scale show many marks of greatness, and his works for the theatre abound in Schubertian inspiration, though they were not, on the whole, successful. However, we have the incidental pieces he wrote for the reputedly very dull play *Rosamunde* to suggest what Schubert might have achieved in this field had he been luckier with his collaborators or, quite simply, had lived longer. As for orchestral music, Schubert's symphonies all have much to delight us, rising as they do to the pathos of No. 8 in B minor (the 'Unfinished') and the nobility of No. 9 (the 'Great' C major).

Franz Schubert   Felix Mendelssohn

For there was a side to Schubert's character far removed from easy ebullience. One of the most marked characteristics of his music is the way it often shifts from major to minor and back again, giving the effect of sudden shadow, of clouds passing across the sun; and in some of Schubert's later music those shadows are deep indeed – in the 'Death and the Maiden' Quartet, for example, or the profoundly moving slow movement of the Quintet in C major. Though he complained little to his friends, Schubert was brought close to despair by the onset of venereal disease when he was only twenty-six, which disfigured him badly for a time; but, young though he was, he found the determination he needed to go on, through his efforts to beautify with his imagination the 'miserable reality' he had to experience.

Happily, Schubert's disease did recede for a time; the convivial evenings began again. And there were days of productive work, when Schubert dismissed callers with an absent-minded 'Hullo, how are you?' before resuming composition. Publishers were at last beginning to recognize Schubert's brilliant qualities, and demanded new works from him, provided they were not too difficult. Suddenly, the shadows fell again, and finally. After an illness of eleven days, Schubert died of typhus. The feelings of his friends were expressed by Moritz von Schwind: 'Schubert is dead, and with him all that we had of the brightest and fairest.'

Felix Mendelssohn (1809–1847)
Mendelssohn was one of the few major composers born to wealth; but although he had every material advantage, he also had a high sense of duty in his chosen profession, and it was overwork, coupled with incessant travel, which led to his sadly premature death.

As the children of a prosperous Jewish banker, who had ideas for their upbringing which were both enlightened and severe, Felix and his sister Fanny were expected to rise at five a.m. every day except Sunday; and on Sunday mornings, in the Mendelssohns' Berlin household, there were domestic concerts at which the most distinguished musicians of the day were invited to make music with the young prodigies. Social proprieties were thought highly important, which perhaps helps to account for the urbanity of Mendelssohn's music.

But, in his best works, Mendelssohn's genius far transcended the niceties of the drawing-room: at sixteen he wrote his superb Octet, at seventeen the marvellous Overture to *A Midsummer Night's Dream*, for which Mendelssohn was to compose a full set of beautiful incidental music in his thirties.

Mendelssohn's education followed the fashion of the time and included a 'Grand Tour' which took him to most places of artistic interest in Europe. The young man recorded his impressions in vivid letters and brilliant sketches, for he was an accomplished writer and artist as well as musician; and he fell particularly in love with London, not least because, having read the romantic novels of Walter Scott, he regarded it as a staging-post on the route to Scotland. As soon as he could, he and a friend travelled north 'with a rake for folk-songs, an eye for the lovely fragrant countryside and a heart for the bare legs of the natives'. The wild, beautiful scenery of Iona and Fingal's Cave made a specially profound impression, and inspired one of the first and finest of tone-poems, the 'Hebrides' Overture, whose main theme was first outlined, characteristically, in a letter home. Another fruit of the journey was the attractive 'Scottish' Symphony, just as the 'Italian' Symphony resulted from Mendelssohn's impressions of Italy.

With Paris and the Parisians, Mendelssohn had little patience; the kind of music he heard at the Opéra might well be transcribed, he said, for 'two flutes and Jew's harp ad lib', and a further source of offence was that the French believed Bach to be 'nothing but a wig stuffed with learning'. Naturally this incensed the brilliant young man who at the age of twenty had rescued Bach's *St Matthew Passion* from oblivion and conducted it twice within a fortnight, to great acclaim, in his native Germany.

It was fortunate indeed that this ardent and expert champion of the then neglected Johann Sebastian should spend the last twelve years of his life as musical director at Leipzig, the city most associated with Bach. Mendelssohn proceeded to make it the musical centre of Germany, establishing the famous Leipzig Conservatoire and refusing to subscribe for a statue of Bach in the town until the necessary funds were forthcoming, as a priority, for music-making and musical education.

From Leipzig, Mendelssohn was free to travel in response to the ceaseless demands for his services as composer and conductor. He visited England no fewer than ten times: Queen Victoria invited him to Windsor and to Buckingham Palace, the Orchestra of the Royal Philharmonic Society would rise and applaud when he entered the hall for a rehearsal, crowds followed him everywhere. Mendelssohn responded with characteristic grace; he even declared that Birmingham was 'delightful'. And it was for Birmingham that he composed the most famous of his oratorios, *Elijah*, which was first performed in the Town Hall there in August 1846. It was a wild success, and Mendelssohn was called upon to conduct it again everywhere; but the effort of completing it, carried out against a background of endless academic and official work, had exhausted the composer. Nevertheless he continued to travel, conduct and lead the unrelenting public life expected of him, until news of the death of his sister Fanny in May 1847 completely prostrated him, and in November of that year he died. He was given the funeral honours of a great statesman. And indeed his importance as a man of musical affairs almost outweighs his achievement as a composer; but the best of his always attractive music shows a deep feeling for realities, as well as for the appearances of civilized life.

Robert Schumann (1810–1856)

If any single individual can be said to embody the idea of a 'romantic' composer, that man must be Schumann. He was born, the son of a bookseller, in Saxony, and he died in a lunatic asylum near Bonn.

Almost from the start, his was a divided soul – torn, in university days at Leipzig, between the study of law and his gift for music; then, soon afterwards, between a career as a composer and as a concert pianist. This second conflict was, however, soon resolved when – in a misguided attempt to gain greater independence of movement in his middle fingers – he permanently damaged the nerves of his right hand through tying up his third finger while he practised. Later on, he seemed to find some balance in a life divided between composition and musical journalism, but towards the end the fantastic imagination which lent such poetry to his music ran wild, and he *saw* the angels and demons he felt were struggling for his soul. His last three years were clouded by the insanity he had long dreaded.

But what poetry there is in the best of his work! And how happy he was for a time, when, at the age of thirty – after a terrible struggle during which his piano teacher, Friedrich Wieck, took him to court – he finally married Wieck's daughter Clara, a fulfilment directly expressed in songs like those of the *Dichterliebe* ('Poet's Love') cycle. Clara, one of the foremost pianists of her time, did all she could to encourage Robert's talent. But here again there was conflict, between her need to practise for long hours and his need for silence to compose; and when they went on tour together, he suffered humiliation. People would ask the famous Clara in Robert's presence, 'Oh, and is your husband a musician too?'

From Clara herself, Robert had nothing but love and encouragement all his life – encouragement to venture into large-scale compositions such as the four symphonies, the opera *Genoveva*, and the symphonic poem *Manfred*, based on Byron; and it was Clara who made the world listen to the exquisite piano pieces which are Schumann's most personal expressions. In *Carnaval*, for example, we encounter the imaginary characters of Florestan, representing romantic ardour, and Eusebius, the dreamer, together with other figures, real and fanciful, who came together in Schumann's mind to fight as the 'Band of David' against the Philistines in the world of art.

For ten years, Schumann ran a journal championing all that was new and exciting in music, using the pseudonymns Florestan and Eusebius as the mood required, and also a third name, Meister Raro; Schumann thought of him as the personification of Reason, and in him he would have liked the 'double nature' of Florestan and Eusebius to merge.

But Schumann was not a man of everyday good sense. By the time he was forty, fears of insanity were growing on him, and he was unable to cope with the practicalities of his job as conductor at Düsseldorf. Life there was painful for the Schumanns, with their family of six children, but it was lightened by the appearance in their home, in 1853, of the young Johannes Brahms. Schumann hailed him boldly as a musical Messiah, 'he who was to come', and it was Brahms who steadfastly supported Clara in the ordeal of Robert's last years. She shared the mental torments of her husband, and it was bitterly hard for her to bear the separation ordained by the authorities of the asylum to which he ultimately had to go. Visits from Brahms were allowed, however, and they were among the few consolations Schumann had at that time. Only at the very end was Clara allowed again to see her husband. 'With a great effort,' she wrote, 'he smiled at me and clasped me in his arms. And I would not give that embrace for all the treasures on earth.'

Johannes Brahms (1833–1897)
Brahms, whose father was a double-bass player, was born in a poor street in Hamburg; and although, long before his death, he was recognized and revered as the great composer he was, he never gave up a simple style of living. Hating collars and ties, he grew an enormous beard which concealed the fact that he often did without them, and in the same way he tried to mask his true character. Perhaps he did not fully understand it himself, for there are contradictions in both the man and his music, which can be lyrical, yet sometimes leaden; soaringly romantic (as in the wonderful Violin Concerto and many great songs), yet boringly academic, as though Brahms felt a great composer just had to be monumental.

The key point in the development of the young Brahms was his introduction to Robert and Clara Schumann in 1853, when he was twenty. It may be that Schumann's exaltation of Brahms gave him an almost oppressive sense of destiny: he felt obliged to follow in the footsteps of Beethoven, and perhaps not surprisingly was unable to complete his own first symphony till he was in his forties.

Robert Schumann   Johannes Brahms

Just as Robert Schumann was the father-figure in the musical life of
Brahms, so Clara Schumann assumed a role in the composer's personal life
which had something of the mother in it. Clara deeply appreciated the
consolation he brought to her and to her children during Schumann's
long illness and after his death, and a deep bond of affection grew up
between them which lasted for the rest of their lives, though after Brahms
settled in Vienna in his late twenties their correspondence became more
spasmodic. It was to Clara that Brahms wrote of his triumphs and dis-
appointments, and she responded by promoting his works whenever she
could: in the case of the D minor Violin Sonata which Brahms wrote in his
fifties, she had such bad pains in her arms that she had to get her daughter
to play the piano part, but struggled to write to Brahms in her own hand
about 'this beautiful sonata'. When Brahms was about forty, a lady called
Elizabeth von Herzogenberg became the composer's confidante and
champion; she was happily married, so there was no question of a
romantic relationship between them. Brahms himself never married,
explaining with customary self-disparagement that if a work of his failed,
he could perfectly well bear it himself, but 'if I had had to go to my wife
and see her questioning eyes anxiously fastened on mine and been
obliged to confess "another fiasco", I couldn't have borne that'.

Just as he was unable to achieve a fully satisfactory relationship with a
woman, so there is a trace of inhibition in the pattern of his musical output.
On the one hand there are the four fine symphonies, two piano concertos,
the violin concerto and 'double' concerto for violin and cello, the *German
Requiem* and the *Tragic Overture*, many wonderful songs and piano solos,
the fine violin sonatas and much other chamber music; on the other there
is a certain amount of lighter music such as the Liebeslieder Waltzes, the

Waltzes Op. 39, and the Hungarian Dances which brought Brahms immense popular success. Perhaps he would have liked to do more in this line, if he had seen his musical destiny differently.

The current of feeling between Brahms and Clara Schumann remained strong to the very end. In March 1896, she had a serious stroke, but managed to scribble a few words as a birthday greeting to Brahms. Not long afterwards she was dead, and Brahms wrote to her daughter Marie, offering any help he could give, and warning her not to misconstrue the 'Four Serious Songs' he had just written – they had no direct bearing on Clara's illness, for he had thought she was improving. But the last of the songs ends with St Paul's words 'Now remains faith, hope, love, these three; but love is the greatest among them.'

Antonin Dvořák (1841–1904)

The Czech composer Dvořák was the first major European composer to forge a musical link between the Old and the New World. In 1892, he left his native Bohemia to accept an invitation to take charge of the National Conservatory of Music in the United States, and one of his most popular works, the stirring Symphony No. 9 in E minor, was written for the New York Philharmonic Orchestra and bears the title 'From the New World'. However, though some people have thought that the beautiful slow movement was based on a Negro spiritual, Dvořák himself denied that he had written American music: much more in evidence was an exile's longing for home. Almost all Dvořák's music is rooted in his own green and wooded land, and often contains echoes of its folk rythms.

But Dvořák took some time to establish his personal style, and he was in his mid-thirties when the Moravian Duets, and the earliest set of Slavonic Dances for piano duets, brought him his first taste of international fame. It has sometimes been said that Dvořák's patriotism was over-diluted with worldly success; but in fact, at every opportunity, he tried to champion the Czech cause, for example by insisting that his Berlin publisher should print the Czech as well as the German titles of his works: 'Do not laugh at my Czech brothers,' he wrote. 'An artist has also his country, in which he must have firm faith, and for which he must have an ardent heart.'

Almost all of Dvořák's vast output of music is easy to listen to. It is full of good tunes and, perhaps because Dvořák himself came of simple country stock, it speaks directly to the heart. There is so much to enjoy that any short list of recommendations is bound to be somewhat arbitrary: however, among the symphonies, Nos. 7, 8 and 9 are perhaps the most immediately appealing; the Cello Concerto in B minor is particularly eloquent and touching – and the String Serenade in E major is very attractive. For home consumption, there are many pieces for solo piano, and pianists can get great enjoyment from the Legends and the two sets of Slavonic Dances for piano duets. There are many fine songs, among which 'Songs My Mother Taught Me' is probably the most

An embodiment of jazz: Duke Ellington

famous; and the well-known aria 'O Silent Moon' from *Russalka* is just one beautiful example of Dvořák's operatic work, to which he attached great importance, again for nationalistic reasons.

Grandeur for its own sake never appealed to Dvořák, and at moments of strain he would turn with relief to two simple passions which absorbed much of his time and attention: the breeding of prize pigeons, and the study of railway engines. The librettist of *Russalka* described how Dvořák would often come to see him soon after seven a.m., 'after his morning round of the Prague railway stations, where he went to look at the locomotives'; and, for all the acclaim he won in New York, Dvořák expressed profound disappointment with the city because there was only one railway station on Manhattan Island. In fact, amid all his American success, Dvořák seemed to find happiness only in the quiet Czech community of Spillsville, Iowa, because there he could play the organ in the little church, and get up at five a.m. to listen to the singing of the birds.

Dvořák was not one of those composers who had to starve for their art: he made a comfortable fortune, though he died (at sixty-three) before he could enjoy the long country retirement he had longed for. But, for those who approached him obsequiously at the height of his fame and success, there was a sharp answer: 'I am just an ordinary Czech musician who does not love exaggerated humility in others, and though I have moved quite enough in the great musical world, I still remain what I have always been, a simple Czech music-maker.'

Richard Wagner (1813–1883)

Wagner probably ought to be known as Richard Geyer, for although he was born in May 1813, the ninth child of Johanna Rosina Wagner, wife of a Leipzig town official, his father may have been the actor Ludwig Geyer, who lived with the Wagners at the time and quickly married Richard's mother when her first husband died of typhoid. If the boy was the son of an actor, it would certainly help to explain his consuming passion for the theatre, which even as a boy exercised on him, he said, 'a fascination like that of a spectre'.

During his somewhat spasmodic schooling, he developed a passion for literature. When he was fifteen he started studying composition, and a performance of Beethoven's *Fidelio* a year later was a crucial factor in deciding his career. Before he was twenty he had composed a good deal of piano and chamber music as well as a symphony in C major, and at that age he began working in various minor opera houses, first as a *répétiteur* (singing coach) and later as conductor. At twenty-three he married a singer, Minna Planer, whose infidelities in the early years of their marriage were to be outmatched by Wagner's own, later on.

In 1839, setting a pattern which was repeated many times, the couple fled from their creditors in the Baltic town of Riga and escaped to England; there then followed three years of struggle and poverty in Paris, where nevertheless Wagner impressed many people with the force and

'Tamla Motown' music from the Jackson Five

Antonin Dvořák

Richard Wagner

charm of his personality. Something of a breakthrough came when his opera *Rienzi*, based on a novel by Bulwer Lytton, was accepted for production in Dresden and staged there with great success in 1842, to be followed by *The Flying Dutchman* in 1843 and *Tannhäuser* in 1845. From 1842, for seven years Wagner knew some security as Capellmeister in the Saxon capital, but in 1848 he made no secret of his sympathy with the revolutionary uprisings of that year, and soon afterwards, through declaring his republican views, was forced into exile. First he made for Weimar, where he was welcomed by Liszt, who later was to champion Wagner's cause to great effect and support the man himself with money, time and time again; but soon Wagner had to leave Germany altogether, and he settled in Zürich. There he found patrons willing to help him, notably the wealthy Otto Wesendonck, whose wife Mathilde conceived a passion for Wagner which was fully reciprocated and was the inspiration of one of Wagner's greatest operas, *Tristan and Isolde*. When the Wesendoncks moved house, Otto went so far as to build a cottage for the Wagners in his grounds, and there, as a member of a quartet which can hardly have been cosy, especially for Minna Wagner, Richard conceived the vast operatic cycle of four operas, *The Ring of the Nibelung*, which was to occupy him for a quarter of a century, as well as *Tristan* and some songs of Frau Wesendonck's poems. In 1858 the charade came to an end when Minna intercepted a letter from her husband to Mathilde. Wagner decamped first to Venice and then to Paris, where *Tannhäuser* was howled off the stage of the Opéra in 1861, and Wagner's debts and despair alike continued to grow.

Rescue came from an unlikely source. In 1864 an eighteen-year-old boy became King Ludwig of Bavaria. Passionately devoted to both Wagner and his music, he at once offered Wagner the chance to realize his artistic dreams at Ludwig's expense in the Bavarian capital, Munich. There the first two operas of the Ring, *The Rhinegold* and *The Valkyrie*, were staged at the Court Opera, as were *Tristan* and *The Mastersingers*. Meanwhile Wagner had begun a passionate liaison with Cosima, wife of his loyal friend and ardent supporter, the conductor and pianist Hans von Bülow. The three of them lived for some time in a lakeside villa provided by King Ludwig, until the scandal became too much, and Wagner once more had to retreat to Switzerland, where for six years he lived near Lucerne. In 1870, after Hans von Bülow divorced his wife, Wagner and Cosima married and on Christmas Day that year Wagner conducted the beautiful *Siegfried Idyll* on the stairs outside his wife's bedroom, where she lay with her first infant son Siegfried.

Disillusioned though he was with Wagner's behaviour, King Ludwig continued to support him in the greatest project of his life, which was to build a Festival Theatre at Bayreuth, specially designed to house the mighty *Ring of the Nibelung*. After many difficulties, and many financial crises, the Theatre opened in August 1876 with the first full performance of the four operas, and the King met Wagner again after eight years, when he attended the third performance of the cycle. On royal money, Wagner was able to build a dream house for himself and Cosima called Wahnfried, but money continued to be a problem. An extravagant style of living, Wagner felt, was vital to him: during the composition of his last opera, the religious epic *Parsifal*, completed in 1882, we read of the scents, silks and bath salts he found indispensable. But although he was perpetually bankrupt, Wagner's fame was now immense throughout Europe: in 1881 *The Ring* was staged in Berlin, and in 1882 in London. But for Wagner himself, the end was near: after a series of heart attacks, he died in Venice in the following year.

Wagner's influence on music was prodigious: he liberated opera from contrived conventions, telling his story with a broad sweep of melody and using the orchestra to supply the essence of the drama; always his own poet, he was clearly a master of the theatre in every aspect. As propaganda, some of Wagner's writings (and they were very extensive) have had tragic consequences, both for the world and his own reputation, notably his scathing attacks on Jews and Jewish art, dictated almost certainly by resentment. He became identified, through his Germanic themes, with the Nazi movement – apologists would say quite wrongly. But whatever the man's beliefs, and whatever his character (Wagner's charm and courage were balanced by unscrupulous egotism), there's no doubt about the thrilling impact of his music, in tune with his belief that music should be 'a power of nature which men perceive but do not understand'.

Giuseppe Verdi (1813–1901)

A man of the soil, Verdi spent almost his whole life near Busseto, a little town in northern Italy. He was born in the village of le Roncole, two miles south-east of the town, and as soon as he began to make money he bought an estate at Sant'Agata just to the north of Busseto, where he farmed and fought off all intrusion into his private life. When Verdi was a boy, northern Italy was dominated by the Austrians: as a man, he was very much identified with the liberation and unification of Italy, becoming a

Member of Parliament for a few years; and one of his finest works is the Requiem Mass he wrote to honour a great literary hero of the Risorgimento, Alessandro Manzoni.

Verdi's parents were not rich, and he was fortunate that a music-loving wine merchant of Busseto, Antonio Barezzi, encouraged his early studies there and in Milan. Bitter tragedy struck the young man in his middle twenties, for his wife Margherita Barezzi, Antonio's daughter, died of meningitis, and their two children also died. At the height of his later triumphs, Verdi never forgave the public for the jeers with which they greeted his early operas, the work of 'a poor young man prostrated and heartbroken by a terrible experience . . . I do not mean to blame them, but I accept their jeers and criticisms on condition that I do not have to be grateful for their applause.'

The breakthrough to public acclaim came when the young Verdi was at his lowest ebb, and a libretto about the persecution of the Jews under King Nebuchadnezzar was thrust upon him. Verdi flung it aside impatiently, but the book fell open at the words 'Fly, thoughts, on gilded wings.' The words haunted Verdi and provided the germ of the great Chorus of Hebrew Slaves in exile in *Nabucco* (produced in 1842), which soon became almost a hymn of Italian patriotism. Verdi's name was made, and the opera houses of Europe vied with each other for a new Verdi work. A brilliant, glamorous life one might suppose, but for Verdi his thirties and forties were, he declared, 'the years in the galleys'. He worked hard, drove hard bargains, and longed to be done with the theatre: 'My mind is always *black*, and will be so till I have finished this career that I abhor.' But Verdi did have his retreat at Sant'Agata, and there a beloved friend, the singer Giuseppina Strepponi, shared his life for twelve years before they finally decided to marry in 1859. When Verdi had to go off to supervise the production of one of his operas, Giuseppina wrote him letters which reveal the integrity of their relationship: 'We are the whole world to each other, and watch with compassion all the human puppets rushing about, climbing up, slipping down, fighting, hiding, reappearing – all trying to put themselves at the head of the social masquerade . . . as long as God leaves us in good health, our simple and modest pleasures and desires will cheer and comfort us even in old age.' Such indeed was the case, and how Verdi resented his absences, particularly the eight months of rehearsals he had to endure in Paris before his *Don Carlos* was staged at the Opéra.

In all, Verdi produced twenty-eight operas; at the age of fifty-seven he completed what is surely the grandest of all grand operas, *Aïda*, commissioned for Cairo, to celebrate the opening of the Suez Canal. Like many of the 'middle-period' Verdi operas – *Rigoletto*, for example, *Il Trovatore*, *La Traviata*, and *A Masked Ball* – it contains many a wonderful melody and exquisitely moving scene, and if Verdi had finally retired at about the age of sixty, which he intended to do, he would still have been a major operatic composer.

Giuseppe Verdi   Peter Ilyich Tchaikovsky

But sixteen years after *Aïda*, thanks to a meeting with a very remarkable poet and musician called Arrigo Boito, what Verdi called the
'Chocolate Project' came to fruition: an opera based on Shakespeare's
Othello, with libretto by Boito. Verdi had at first done everything in his
power to put Boito off, but Boito had tact as well as persistence, and between them the two men produced a thrilling dramatic masterpiece.
Another six years of reluctant hard work eventually resulted in what is
perhaps an even greater masterpiece, again conceived in collaboration
with Boito: the comic-opera *Falstaff*, which Verdi completed at the age of
eighty.

After that he was to live on for another eight years, at once a national
hero and the 'old bear' of Sant'Agata, enduring for the last three years of
his life the loneliness which followed the death of Giuseppina, and
resolutely refusing all requests to write his memoirs: 'It is quite enough
for the world that it should have had to put up with my music for all these
years. *Never* will I condemn it to read my prose!'

Verdi died after having at last been persuaded to move, for the final
few months of his life, to the comfort of a hotel in Milan. The outer crust
which protected him from the world was hard; but the world saw through
it, to revere and love the great man inside.

Peter Ilyich Tchaikovsky (1840–1893)
There are few composers who have consciously put quite so much of their
soul on to manuscript paper as Tchaikovsky. Even as a child, born of
middle-class parents in the provincial town of Votkinsk, he was intensely
emotional and extremely sensitive to criticism from those he loved: his
governess described him as a 'child of glass'. When he was twelve he was
taken to see Mozart's opera *Don Giovanni*, and at once he formed an inner
determination to live for music. But Tchaikovsky graduated in law, and

he worked for a while in the Ministry of Justice before going to study at the St Petersburg Conservatoire at the age of twenty-three; only three years later, he was appointed Professor of Harmony at the Conservatoire in Moscow.

Soon he imagined he was in love with a singer called Désirée Artot, and thought of marrying her. However, she ran off with a Spanish baritone – perhaps fortunately, because Tchaikovsky was probably homosexual, and when he did marry he brought about the greatest disaster of his life. His own emotional problems gave him a sharp appreciation of frustrated passion, and this unhappy experience was expressed in his scores over and over again, for example in the fine concert overture *Romeo and Juliet*. When the subject of the star-crossed lovers was suggested to Tchaikovsky, he knew at once it was ideal for him: 'If I were asked the question "Have you ever known the happiness of requited love?", my answer would be "No, no, no!" he wrote. 'But ask me whether I am capable of comprehending the immense force of love, and I will answer "Yes, yes, yes!" Have I not, in my music, done my best to express the torments and felicities of love?'

The *Romeo and Juliet* overture failed at its first performance, and Tchaikovsky had a hard long struggle for recognition as a composer. For the head of the Moscow Conservatoire, Nicholas Rubinstein, he wrote the now famous and enormously popular First Piano Concerto in B flat minor; but after he'd played through the first movement, Rubinstein rounded on the astonished composer in fury, denouncing the work as bad, trivial, worthless, vulgar and unplayable. Strangely enough, it was in America that Tchaikovsky's music first found an enthusiastic public: in October 1875, von Bülow played the First Piano Concerto in Boston and had to encore the finale. Tchaikovsky was delighted, and of course all the more disillusioned with his own countrymen.

A commission for the ballet *Swan Lake* from the Bolshoi Theatre encouraged Tchaikovsky for a time, but the first performance was appallingly bungled, and indeed the beautiful score was not adequately performed until after the composer's death. Into this work and the two other full-length ballets, *The Nutcracker* and *The Sleeping Beauty*, he put some of his very finest music: Tchaikovsky did not see why ballet music had to be trivial, and his serious approach to the medium set the stage for the great international success of the Russian Ballet in the early years of the twentieth century.

Soon after the *Swan Lake* fiasco, a 'fairy godmother' came into Tchaikovsky's life: a wealthy widow, Nadezhda von Meck, who so admired his work that she paid off his debts and awarded him an annuity which gave him freedom to compose, on condition that they should never meet. An ideal arrangement for one of Tchaikovsky's temperament; but soon after the arrangement was made, a persistent former pupil threatened to kill herself unless Tchaikovsky promised to marry her. In July 1877 the marriage took place. It nearly cost Tchaikovsky his reason, for his wife proved to be both a nymphomaniac and a philistine. During a long breakdown Tchaikovsky came near to suicide. But his brother and Nadezhda von Meck stood by him, until that lady, in 1890, decided for family reasons that she could no longer continue her support of the composer, which made Tchaikovsky feel, as he told his brother, that 'the last hope of any happiness I may have been intended by fate to enjoy has disappeared'. In 1893 he drank a glass of unboiled water, and thus caused his own death from cholera.

Tchaikovsky wrote a great deal of music of many kinds, much of which is extremely popular today. In his operas, Tchaikovsky was able to use his own bitter experiences objectively, to lend conviction to his stage characters; but there's no doubt that the well-known and much-loved Fourth, Fifth and Sixth Symphonies give expression to his own personal emotions. He and Nadezhda von Meck called the Fourth 'our symphony', and Tchaikovsky, at her request, supplied her with a scenario, describing how the hammer blows of fate strike at a man over and over again, as soon as he sees a distant prospect of happiness. Subjective melancholy, however, was by no means the whole of Tchaikovsky, who was a master craftsman of the highest class, an ardent Russian patriot, and capable at times of forgetting his own troubles. The message of the tumultuous festivity which ends the Fourth Symphony reads thus, in Tchaikovsky's own words: 'There is *still* such a thing as joy. Rejoice in the happiness of others, and it will still be possible for you to live.'

Igor Stravinsky (1882–1971)

Paradoxically, a love of Tchaikovsky's music had great influence on the objectively intellectual Stravinsky, whose long life began near St Petersburg in Russia and ended in New York. All along, Stravinsky never ceased experimenting with his art, changing his style so radically at various points in his career that it is sometimes hard to believe that such very different works came from the pen of the same man.

An interest in innovation seems to have awakened early in Stravinsky, for he remembered thinking as a boy of eight that someone must have invented the scale of C major, and so he, Stravinsky, could invent something else. At about the same age he attended a performance of Tchaikovsky's *The Sleeping Beauty*, which made an enormous impression on him. His father, an opera singer, had no wish for his son to be connected with music and the theatre, but as soon as he could, Igor abandoned law studies at the University and worked at composition with Rimsky-Korsakov as his guide.

Stravinsky's first significant success came in 1909 when a short orchestral piece called *Fireworks* attracted the attention of the great ballet impresario Serge Diaghilev. Diaghilev soon commissioned Stravinsky to compose music for *The Firebird*, a legendary Russian tale, and the first performance of this ballet in June 1910 made Stravinsky's name on the international scene. This is an opulent score, full of picturesque colour.

Petrushka, staged in 1912, had much more incisive music; and *The Rite of Spring*, with its barbaric rhythms and spiky themes, caused a riot when it was first seen in the following year.

During the upheavals of the First World War and the Russian Revolution, Stravinsky and his family spent most of their time in Switzerland, where he could no longer call on a vast orchestra; but changing his style to suit the limited forces at his disposal, he wrote a witty and moving masterpiece, *The Soldier's Tale*, which showed, among other things, the influence of jazz.

Another stylistic change, a very important one, came in 1920 when Diaghilev asked Stravinsky to adapt music by the eighteenth-century Italian composer Pergolesi for a ballet called *Pulcinella*. 'It was', wrote Stravinsky later, 'my discovery of the past'; and this discovery led to a whole series of 'neo-classical' scores, distinguished by a spare purity of style, such as *Oedipus Rex* and *Persephone*. Though Stravinsky lived mainly in France from 1920 to 1939, American interest in his work was steadily growing through this period, and it was for the Boston Symphony Orchestra that he wrote his *Symphony of Psalms* (1930), a marvellous choral and orchestral symphony on material close to Stravinsky's heart. 'I composed it', he wrote, 'in a state of religious and musical ebullience.' But although Stravinsky had returned to the religious beliefs he had abandoned as a youth, and religious themes were to become increasingly important to him, it would be the greatest mistake to read into Stravinsky's music an expression of his own feelings. 'Music', he wrote, 'is by its very nature powerless to express anything at all, whether a feeling, an attitude of mind, a psychological mood, a phenomenon of nature, etc. . . . music is the sole domain in which man *realizes the present* . . . it is given to us with the sole purpose of establishing an order in things, including – and particularly – the co-ordination between man and time. To be put into practice, the indispensable single requirement is *construction*.'

This determination to write 'absolute' music uninfluenced by extraneous emotional concepts led to an increasing austerity of style; during his life in America from the beginning of the Second World War until his death, Stravinsky moved on from the neo-classicism of the Symphony in C and the opera *The Rake's Progress* (1951) to twelve-tone compositions in the manner pioneered by Schoenberg, apparently aiming at an ever-increasing concentration of musical meaning. There was, however, no lack of human feeling, for some of the most terse and abstract of Stravinsky's later statements were made in honour of such men as Dylan Thomas, President Kennedy, Aldous Huxley and T. S. Eliot, and Stravinsky's great interest in religion was reflected in such works as the cantata *Abraham and Isaac*.

Stravinsky's later music is difficult and somewhat inaccessible, but, when examined closely, it is often seen to contain more musical thought in the space of six minutes than many a romantic symphony contains in sixty. Hard work, perhaps; but worth it, if you want to come to terms with

Ignor Stravinsky   Claude Debussy

one of the greatest musical minds of the twentieth century, and, for all
Stravinsky's protestations to the contrary, one of the most expressive.

Claude Debussy (1862–1918)

A leading authority on Debussy, Edward Lockspeiser, has described his
music as 'an art merging the real and the unreal with uncanny precision',
a phrase which is a precise summing-up of the composer's special quality.

Debussy's life was centred around the French capital: he was born at
St Germain, not far away, and died in Paris while it was under German
bombardment in the First World War. As a young child he never went
to school. He was educated by his mother, who adored him; and this
private upbringing led to a social unease which never quite left him and
which made life hard at the Paris Conservatoire, where he went at the age
of ten, and was to remain for some twelve years. Challenged by a professor
about his dissonant harmonies and asked 'What rule do you follow?',
Debussy replied, 'My pleasure', thus foreshadowing the highly individual
sensuousness of much of his music. In his last years at the Conservatoire,
Debussy's horizons were broadened by travels in the company of Nadezhda
von Meck, Tchaikovsky's great friend and patron, who engaged the young
man for three summers as a teacher for her children; and in 1884 he won
the Conservatoire's supreme prize, the Prix de Rome, with his cantata *The
Prodigal Son*. A friend told him the news while Debussy was standing on one
of the bridges of Paris, enjoying the view. 'I can assure you that all my
pleasure vanished,' wrote Debussy later. 'I saw in a flash the boredom,
the vexations inevitably incident to the slightest official recognition. I
was no longer *free*.'

Debussy was supposed to spend three years in Rome as a result of win-
ning the prize, but although he stayed in Italy long enough to meet Liszt –
and also Verdi, who was planting salads at Sant'Agata – he returned to

Paris a year early, and there found himself grappling with the all-pervading influence of Wagner. It was some time before the authentic Debussy
voice was heard, but it emerged clearly in the dreamy *Prélude à l'Après-
Midi d'un Faune*, completed in 1894, the String Quartet of 1893 (with its
echoes of the gamelan orchestras which had delighted him at a Great
International Exhibition of 1889), and in the opera *Pelléas et Mélisande*
(based on the play by Maurice Maeterlinck), which occupied Debussy
from 1893 to 1902, when it was staged at the Opéra Comique. The
atmosphere of *Pelléas* is transparent, mysterious and elusive, concerned
with the half-lights of a legendary world, at once luminous and threaten-
ing. There is nothing else like it to be seen on the operatic stage, and
although there were adverse criticisms, it attracted packed houses both
at its first presentation in Paris and at London's Covent Garden in 1909.

Before *Pelléas* reached the stage, there had been a devastating quarrel
with Maeterlinck which almost led to a duel: it was all through a mis-
understanding. But Debussy's actions were liable to cause misunderstand-
ings, even with close friends. After living with a pretty, vivacious blonde
called Gabrielle Dupont for about ten years, he married, in 1899, Rosalie
('Lily') Texier. In 1904, Lily shot herself when Debussy left her for the
wealthy Emma Bardac, wife of a financier; Debussy's reasons remain
somewhat unclear, but the action cost him many friends, quite apart
from causing a great scandal in Paris.

Debussy lost himself in the creation of his great three-part symphony
La Mer ('The Sea'), first performed in 1905, the year which brought
marriage to Emma after the birth of a beloved daughter nicknamed
Chou-Chou, for whom Debussy wrote his enchanting piano suite *Children's Corner*. Debussy's piano music consists of a large number of delicate
and highly evocative miniatures, both tantalizing and satisfying – a
sensation conveyed, too, in the shadowy forms of the orchestral works
entitled *Nocturnes* ('Nuages', 'Fêtes' and 'Sirènes'), and *Images* ('Gigues',
'Ibéria' and 'Rondes de Printemps'). Like so many other major artists of
the day, Debussy contributed to the Russian ballet of Diaghilev, with the
score for *Jeux* ('Games'), first staged in 1913 and choreographed by
Nijinsky in the style of a game of tennis. May 1911 saw the production of
an interesting stage work, *The Martyrdom of St Sebastian*, based on a miracle
play by Gabriele D'Annunzio, in which Debussy's natural interest in the
mystical found expression; and, during all this period, Debussy was for
ever working on new ideas for operas, none of which came to completion,
perhaps because, from 1909 till his death nine years later, his health was
increasingly undermined by cancer. His output became more spasmodic,
and Debussy became more and more depressed: 'I fight against illness
and against myself. I feel a nuisance to everyone.' The funeral took place
against the distant rumbling of German guns; as it passed, someone in the
street was heard to remark, 'They say he was a musician.'

The importance of Debussy's place in the development of music has
been much discussed. Was he the supreme *musicien français* ('French

musician'), as he signed himself, expressing in a superlative way the characteristic national genius for lucidity, or was he one of music's great pioneers, assisting at the breakdown of the tonal system, and helping to create a new harmonic world? Perhaps he was both. But whatever the answers to these questions, there is no doubt that Debussy helped us all in a unique way (as he himself put it) to 'feel the supreme and moving beauty of the spectacle to which nature invites her ephemeral guests'.

Gustav Mahler (1860–1911)

In the years since the Second World War a great vogue has grown up for the music of Mahler, who was born in a village on the borders of Bohemia and died in Vienna at the age of fifty. It may be that a generation which has experienced much horrific violence finds its unease reflected in Mahler's feverish moods; the composer's desire to find escape in religious ecstasy and the simplicity of childhood is also echoed in our troubled times.

Mahler had an unhappy childhood himself, with parents who did not agree, but at fifteen he escaped to the Conservatoire at Vienna. Although he composed whenever time allowed throughout his life, it was as an operatic conductor, the most remarkable of his generation, that he earned his living. After gaining experience in minor appointments, he went to Budapest as Director of the Royal Opera in 1885, where he remained for six years, attracting the enthusiastic support of Brahms, who told his friends that if they wanted to hear *Don Giovanni* performed properly they must go to Budapest. The influence of Brahms counted for much in Mahler's eventual appointment to the State Opera in Vienna, which took place in 1897 after a successful period in Hamburg. For ten years Mahler ruled the Vienna Opera, bringing brilliant new standards to operatic production there; he drove himself and everyone else with a relentless fanaticism which inspired his admirers but generated growing resentment in other quarters. In 1907 he was forced to resign, and thereafter much of his working life was spent in New York, where he had great success with the New York Philharmonic and at the Metropolitan Opera House.

The influence of country song and dance and of nature is strongly felt in Mahler's music, particularly in *Songs of a Wayfarer* and some of the earlier of his nine completed symphonies, which make use of voices as well as instruments. All Mahler's symphonies are long; No. 3 in fact holds the symphonic endurance record, taking two hours to perform. However, they are all full of marvellous ideas and beautiful melodies. No. 4 uses material from a collection of naïve folk songs called *The Boy's Magic Horn* and is one of the most lyrical and immediately attractive of the symphonies; No. 5 contains a moving Adagietto and, like No. 6 (profoundly pessimistic) and No. 7 (Mahler's most positive symphony), is a purely instrumental work. No. 8 shows Mahler working on musical canvas which requires a huge choir and orchestra: a setting of the ancient hymn 'Veni Creator Spiritus', together with part of Goethe's *Faust*, it has come

Gustav Mahler   Arnold Schoenberg

to be known as the 'Symphony of a Thousand', and very thrilling it can
be. No. 9 is, in the opinion of many, one of Mahler's very finest works, as is
The Song of The Earth, a setting of fatalistic Chinese poems about love, life
and death, completed towards the end of Mahler's life. Perhaps his
greatest gratification came with the huge success of his Eighth Symphony
at Munich in September 1910.

Mahler was fortunate in his wife Alma, whom he married in 1902: she
was a wonderful source of support to him, and was to become his expert
and ardent champion after he died. But they endured a terrible tragedy
when the elder of their two daughters died at the age of five in 1907, an
event which depressed Mahler profoundly. Born a Jew, he had become a
Roman Catholic in 1895, and was deeply religious; but if we are to judge
from his music, this seems to have made almost more unbearable his grief
for the world's lost innocence.

Arnold Schoenberg (1874–1951)

Schoenberg – who was born in Vienna and died in Los Angeles – was a
pivotal figure in the development of twentieth-century music. As a boy
he studied the violin and cello and composed works in the conventional
popular idiom of the day: he had little formal teaching, so it was through
his own intellectual brilliance and originality that he evolved revolutionary methods of composition.

His *Verklärte Nacht* ('Transfigured Night', 1899) and a set of songs first
performed in 1900 caused considerable controversy. But they merely
explored processes already developed by Wagner and Debussy: 'key'
had ceased to be of great importance, and music no longer had to begin
from a home-base to which it must ultimately return. Discords, once
thought to need 'resolving' into concords, existed for their own value:
it was, as Schoenberg put it, the 'emancipation of dissonance'.

But it was not until 1908 that Schoenberg made a decisive break with
the tonal system, when he published his *Piano Pieces*, Op. 11, without key

signature. The *Five Orchestral Pieces* of 1909, and the famous *Pierrot Lunaire* of 1912, in which a narrator declaims, in a kind of song-speech, a sequence of poems with accompaniment for five instruments, also belong to this revolutionary period. The outrage felt by the musical public broke into open riot at a concert in Vienna in March 1913 when works by Schoenberg and his two principal pupils, Webern and Berg, were played: the police had to be called in to empty the hall. All the more credit, then, to Sir Henry Wood, the original conductor of London's Promenade Concerts, who introduced *Five Orchestral Pieces* to Britain in 1912.

By 1923, Schoenberg's thinking had led him to take another decisive step in the technique of composition; having already abandoned the sheet-anchor of conventional harmony, he needed a new unifying principle for music, which he found in the 'tone-row'. The first Schoenberg works to employ this technique were the *Five Piano Pieces*, Op. 23, and the *Serenade*, Op. 24. He also made a start in the 1920s on his important opera *Moses and Aaron*, which he did not complete until shortly before his death. The choice of this story is significant for Schoenberg; it tells how a man like Moses can glimpse the Promised Land, but is held back through having in him something of Aaron, who made the Golden Calf, a totem which 'does not express thought, but dominates it'. *Moses and Aaron* is, of course, also a Jewish story, and although in 1921 Schoenberg had renounced the Jewish religion, he embraced it again when the Nazis dismissed him in 1933 from his Berlin professorship.

Schoenberg first went to France, and then to America, where he worked briefly in New York and Boston before being offered a professorial chair in Southern California. He became an American citizen in 1940, and exercised every bit as powerful an influence on the American musical scene as he had done in Europe. But for all the importance of his teaching work, it was art and not theory which came first for Schoenberg; his ideas grew out of what he felt were the problems of practical composition: 'The accent does not lie so much on twelve tones but on the art of composing.' He was a man of great integrity who followed to the limits the dictates of his own artistic conscience. Yet Schoenberg also realized that his way was not necessarily for every man, and those who find the serial route stony may take heart from another surprising Schoenberg dictum: 'There is still a lot of good music to be written in C major.'

Edward Elgar (1857–1934)

Born within sight of the ancient Cathedral of Worcester in the English West Midlands, Elgar somehow personifies the English country gentleman of a bygone age. But he was much more besides: the first major British-born composer since Purcell, and the first to achieve a big international reputation. When Elgar's beautiful oratorio *The Dream of Gerontius* was performed at Düsseldorf in May 1902, Richard Strauss hailed him as a great composer and announced that he would conduct Elgar's overture *Cockaigne*, that distillation of Edwardian London, in

Berlin. As far as British audiences were concerned, the breakthrough had
already come three years earlier, with the first performance at the St
James's Hall in London of the 'Enigma' *Variations on an Original Theme for
Orchestra*, which was an immediate success.

Elgar dedicated the 'Enigma' Variations to 'My Friends Pictured
Within', and on one level it is a series of musical portraits of the people
who were closest to him, almost all country-town characters like himself,
whose friendship dated from Elgar's long formative years as a competent,
all-round provincial musician – years which extended into early middle
age. At the age of thirty-two he married and moved with his wife briefly
to London, where he made a swift popular success with the universally
known *Salut d'Amour*.

There was plenty of humour in Elgar's character; he was fond of practical jokes, enjoyed tinkering with chemical appliances, and loved bicycles
and motor-cars and the undemanding commerce of country life. But
in the same year that brought the success of the 'Enigma', Clara Butt
sang Elgar's *Sea Pictures* before Queen Victoria at Balmoral Castle – and
Elgar was on the way to a knighthood, a baronetcy, and ten years as
Master of the King's Musick. In the role of Musical Laureate of the
British Empire, he could turn out the most jingoistic of patriotic songs –
such as 'Land of Hope and Glory' (actually the middle section of one of
Elgar's *Pomp and Circumstance* marches), which still brings the house
down at the Last Night of London's Promenade Concerts – and much
more in the same vein.

But there was quite another Elgar too, as we learn from, for example,
two glowing symphonies, and the soulful Violin Concerto, which bore
another enigmatic inscription: *Aquí está encerrada el alma de . . .* ('Here lies
buried the soul of . . .'). Of whom? Of Elgar himself? Then there is much
delicate incidental music, and the oratorios; above all, the sombre beauties
of *Gerontius*, based on the poem by Cardinal Newman about the passage
of a human soul from this world to the next; and, most moving of all to
some people, the Cello Concerto of 1919, full of autumnal sadness, an
epitaph, it would seem, for the world that perished in the First World
War.

With the death of his beloved wife in 1920, Elgar stopped composing
major works, gave up as much as he could of life in London, and retired
once more to the country: 'The old artistic "striving" world exists for
me no more,' he wrote. But there was still the consolation of friendship
in these last years. George Bernard Shaw, who specially admired the
symphonic study *Falstaff*, written in 1913, was one sympathetic spirit:
he was rewarded with the dedication of Elgar's *Severn Suite* for brass band,
written in 1930, which Shaw declared 'will secure my immortality when
all my plays are dead and damned and forgotten!' And towards the end
of his life Elgar had the gratification of recording his Violin Concerto with
the sixteen-year-old Yehudi Menuhin, whose intuitive artistry so impressed Elgar that, after the first thirty bars or so, he stopped the rehearsal

Edward Elgar   Charles Ives

with the characteristic words 'That's enough for today. It couldn't be
done better. Let's go to the races.' Edward Elgar, English gentleman,
did not care to reveal, except to a very few choice friends, the sensitive
soul within.

Charles Ives (1874–1954)

The American composer Charles Ives, who was born at Danbury, Connecticut, and died in New York, was unquestionably one of the most
remarkable musical pioneers of the early twentieth century; but the fact
is that his work was more or less unknown to the public until after he had
ceased composing, and only in recent years has it become clear that in his
experiments with dissonance and quarter-tones, atonality, polyrhythms
(using two or more rhythms simultaneously) and polyharmony (in an
organ piece of 1898 he superimposed the chord of D minor on the chord
of C major), he was certainly as advanced as European contemporaries
like Schoenberg and Stravinsky and in some ways was ahead of them. He
anticipated by more than half a century the composers of our own day
who allow for an interchange of instruments in some works, and make
certain passages optional, the idea being to involve the performer in the
creative process.

Charles Ives's father, a bandmaster, was keenly interested in experiment himself and made a machine for producing quarter-tones. So at an
early age Ives absorbed an uninhibited attitude to music coupled with a
strong feeling for its popular American forms. At the age of twelve he
played drums in his father's band at village concerts, graduating rapidly
to piano, cornet and organ; he went to Yale University to study music,
where (not surprisingly) his experimental compositions outraged the
professors. Ives's motive, however, was not to shock; it was to discover a

valid American way of composing: 'We have listened too long to the courtly muses of Europe,' wrote Ralph Waldo Emerson in 1837, and Ives said an emphatic 'Amen' to that. Folk tunes and hymns, popular marches and patriotic songs, all found their way into his scores, which bear titles such as *Washington's Birthday, Fireman's Parade on Main Street, Children's Day at a Camp Meeting* (this last was a violin sonata). Perhaps his most imposing and interesting single work is the 'Concord' Sonata, which consists of portraits of literary heroes who were active in the town of Concord, Massachusetts, between 1840 and 1860 – Emerson, Hawthorne, the Alcotts and Thoreau: the last movement requires the piano to be played with a strip of wood laid across the keys.

It was typical of the way things went with Ives that the Concord Sonata was completed in 1915, published (at the composer's expense) in 1922, and not performed until 1939. Recognition, even then, was slow in coming to Ives: in 1947 he was awarded the Pulitzer Prize for his Third Symphony, written in 1911.

This extraordinary man, in fact, went on turning out great quantities of music without apparent hope of performance, while making a living from a mutual life insurance company which he formed with a friend in 1909 and ran until 1930, when ill-health forced him to retire from business – and from composing, too, since he had a diabetic condition which made it hard for him to hold a pen. Almost as adept with words as he was with music, Ives expressed thus the value of his everyday work: 'My business experience revealed life to me in many aspects that I might have missed. In it one sees tragedy, nobility, meanness, high aims, low aims, brave hopes, faint hopes, great ideals, no ideals, and one is able to watch these work their inevitable destiny.' Apart from his business life, Ives was highly articulate as an American citizen, advocating, among other things, the use of the Referendum to settle major Federal issues: he felt passionately about politics in the broadest sense, and insisted on democratic rights for his music too. Some of his songs, he knew and said, were unsingable: 'An excuse', wrote Ives, 'is that a song has a few rights the same as ordinary citizens . . . if it happens to feel like flying where humans cannot fly . . . to scale mountains that are not there, who shall stop it?'

Ives lived a quiet private life with his wife (named Harmony), seldom attended concerts, did not read the daily papers – it is clear that he was a visionary who concerned himself only with the major issues of human life. A prophetic utterance of Ives provides us with a fascinating final impression in our gallery of great composers: 'The Future of music may not lie entirely with music itself, but rather in the way it encourages and extends, rather than limits, the aspirations and ideals of the people, in the way it makes itself a part with the finer things that humanity does and dreams of.'

10
What Next?

Many composers of our own time have veered away from established musical forms and musical instruments towards the ambiguities which have always belonged to music at its deepest level. The impersonality of electronic instruments – the kind of work being done, for example, by the B.B.C. Radiophonic Workshop in London – may seem at first a little worrying, in that it might suggest a tendency to do without the human element as far as possible. But experiment with the electronic generation of sound has given creators of music a new kind of freedom: the sounds produced are not necessarily associated with any particular instrument or with the tradition thus implied – they can be evocative in quite a different way, opening our ears to exciting new areas of awareness. It's interesting how often producers of significant plays for the theatre and for broadcasting, and directors of feature films, nowadays turn to electronic means for the atmospheric music they require. The less the theme of the play is tied to some material place or time – the more it is concerned with the illusions and realities of the mind – the more it will need music free to express dreams rather than appearances, music no longer tied to conventions which mark it as belonging to this or that period, appealing to this or that kind of society.

Where will music go from here? No one can foretell, any more than the medieval monk could foresee the operas of Mozart.

Ours is a time of questioning in almost every area of life. Almost every old assumption, almost every loyalty, is being called in question, and much confusion of values is the result. But it may be that such a period of chaos is essential – that through it we are being driven once again to ask basic questions about the nature of the human spirit and the meaning of our life on earth. Such problems cannot be solved in words, only through mysteries; and whatever happens we can still share what Joseph Addison once called 'the greatest good we mortals know', the only universal language, the mysterious Magic of Music.

For Further Reference

BERNSTEIN, Leonard. *The Infinite Variety of Music*. New York, Simon & Schuster, 1966; London, Weidenfeld & Nicolson, 1968.

BIANCOLLI, Louis, and MANN, William, editors. *Analytical Concert Guide*. London, Cassell; Westport, Connecticut, Greenwood Press.

CLARKE, Mary, and CRISP, Clement. *Ballet: An Illustrated History*. London, A. & C. Black; New York, Universe Books, 1973.

GROVE, George. *Dictionary of Music and Musicians*. 10 vols. London, Macmillan (new edition pending); New York, St Martin's Press, 1954.

HINDLEY, Geoffrey, editor. *Larousse Encyclopaedia of Music*. London, Hamlyn, 1971.

HUGHES, Gervase, and VAN THAL, Herbert, editors. *Music Lover's Companion*. London, Eyre & Spottiswoode.

ILLING, Robert. *Pergamon Dictionary of Musicians and Music*. 2 vols. Oxford, Pergamon; Elmsford, N.Y., Pergamon, 1963–4.

KOBBE, Gustave. *Complete Opera Book*. Edited by the Earl of Harewood. New York, Putnam, 1963, and London, 1969.

LANG, Paul Henry. *A Hundred Years of Music in America*. New York, Schirmer, 1961.

LAWSON, Joan. *A History of Ballet and Its Makers*. London, Dance Books, 1973.

Master Musicians Series. London, Dent; New York, Farrar, Straus & Giroux.

ROBERTSON, Alec, and STEVENS, Denis, editors. *Pelican History of Music*. 3 vols. London, Pelican, 1965–71.

ROSENTHAL, Harold, and WARRACK, John, editors. *Concise Oxford Dictionary of Opera*. Oxford University Press, 1972.

SCHOLES, Percy A. *Concise Oxford Dictionary of Music*. Edited by John Owen Ward. Oxford University Press, 1968.

SCHOLES, Percy A. *Oxford Companion to Music*. Edited by John Owen Ward. Oxford University Press, 1970.

VON WESTERMAN, Gerhart. *Concert Guide*. Translated by Cornelius Cardew. London, Sphere, 1968.

VON WESTERMAN, Gerhart. *Opera Guide*. Translated by Anne Ross. London, Sphere, 1968; New York, Dutton, 1968.

Notes on the Illustrations, and Acknowledgments

Where the following abbreviations appear in the notes, they are intended to indicate the locations of pictures, and to acknowledge permission to reproduce photographs that the museums, art galleries, and other institutions (or specifically their governing bodies) have granted in cases where they hold the copyright.

BM: The Trustees of the British Museum, London
RTH: The Radio Times Hulton Picture Library
V & A: The Trustees of the Victoria and Albert Museum, London

Jacket FRONT Photo: *Radio Times.* BACK Original design based on instruments supplied by Boosey & Hawkes. Photo: Christopher Ridley.

8–9 Wood engraving in the Orchesographie de Thoinot Arbeau (Jehan Tabouret), Langres, 1588. Photo: RTH.

12 Photo: RTH.

15 ABOVE Photo: David Farrell. LEFT Photo: Camera Press.

17 Stele, pre-Saitic period, 'The Singer of Amon'. Louvre, Paris. Photo: Giraudon.

18 Photo: Robert Harding.

20 ABOVE Photo: Francis Goodman; Camera Press. LEFT Photo: RTH.

23 Photo: Denis de Marney.

25 Photo: Gerald Wilson; Barnaby.

26 Photo: Barnaby.

30–1 Photo: British Travel.

32 V & A.

35 Photo: Robert Harding.

36 Photo: Robert Harding.

39 Clavichord by Bathold Fritz, Brunswick, 1751. Viola d'amore by Lambert, Paris, 1772. Both V & A.

40 LEFT to RIGHT Theorbo by Matteo Buechenberg, Rome, 1619; chittarone by Buechenberg, Rome, 1614; theorbo, Italian 17th century (neck and crude bridge of later date). V & A.

43 Peasant-type tabor made in Pall Mall, London, 19th century. V & A. B.B.C. radiophonic workshop: B.B.C. copyright photograph.

45 French 16th century. Musée Instrumental, Brussels. From *Les Instruments de Musique dans l'Art et l'Histoire* by R. Bragard and F. J. de Hen; Albert De Visscher, Editor, Brussels.

46–7 From a late 13th-century MS. in Latin and French. MS. Douce 180, p. 26. Bodleian Library.

48 ABOVE Photo: Robert Harding. BELOW Photo: Sybil Sassoon; Robert Harding.

50 Facsimile of Tropus Tutillo's *Modie Cantandus* from MS. 378 at St Gall, 10th century. RIGHT 16th-century carol. Both photos: RTH.

52   From the autograph MS. of *Das Wohltemperirtes Klavier, c.* 1744, and RIGHT of *Siegfried, c.* 1875. Both photos: RTH.

54   Photo: Henmar Press, New York.

58   Photo: RTH.

67   Anita Völkki as Brünnhilde and David Ward as Wotan at the Royal Opera House, London. Photo: Donald Southern.

68   Ballet by Frederick Ashton, performed by the Royal Ballet Company at the Royal Opera House, London, 1968, with Rudolph Nureyev and Antoinette Sibley. Photo: Dominic.

71   Photo: G. Obrezkov, Moscow; Camera Press.

72   Photo: Len Sirman Press, Geneva; Camera Press.

73   From *The Musical Express.* Photo: Fin Costello, London.

74   Photo: RTH.

77   Photo: RTH.

79   *A Concert*, painted *c.* 1488 by Lorenzo Costa. National Gallery, London.

81   Photo: Camera Press.

82–3   *Children Making Music*, painted 1629 by Jan Molenaer. National Gallery, London.

84   ABOVE Maypole on Burchett's Green. Photo: Jon Gardey; Robert Harding. BELOW May 7th Cadre School, Peking. Photo: Tim Magarry; Robert Harding.

87   *A Young Woman Playing the Harpsichord to a Young Man*, painted *c.* 1569 by Jan Steen. National Gallery, London.

91   *A Musical Conversation*, drawn *c.* 1760 by Marcellus Laroon. Duke of Bedford Collection. Paul Mellon Foundation.

93   From a daguerreotype, 1840. Photo: RTH.

98   Caruso (1873–1921). Photo: RTH.

101   Rehearsal for B.B.C.2 programme *Show of the Week*, May 1968. B.B.C. copyright photograph.

102   Photo: John D. Drysdale; Camera Press.

105   Photo: David Farrell.

106   Aldeburgh Festival, 1963. Photo: Camera Press.

109   London production. Photo: Les Wilson; Camera Press.

110   Wladimiro Ganzarolli as Guglielmo and Josephine Veasey as Dorabella at the Royal Opera House, London, 1968. B.B.C. copyright photograph.

112   LEFT National Portrait Gallery, London. RIGHT Photo: RTH.

114   LEFT and RIGHT Photos: RTH.

118   LEFT Photo: Camera Press. RIGHT Photo: RTH.

121   LEFT Staatsbibliothek, Berlin. RIGHT Bildarchiv Foto Marburg.

125   LEFT and RIGHT Photos: RTH.

127   B.B.C. copyright photograph.

128   Photo: David Redfern.

130   LEFT and RIGHT Photos: RTH.

133   LEFT and RIGHT Photos: RTH.

137   LEFT and RIGHT Photos: RTH.

140   LEFT Photo: RTH. RIGHT B.B.C. copyright photograph.

143   LEFT Photo: RTH. RIGHT Photo: U.S. Information Service, London.

Index

Page numbers in *italic* type indicate illustrations.